세미오시스 연구총서 01

Semiosis of African American Religion

Its Symbols and Meanings Since Slavery

Mikyung Ahn

HUFS Press

이 도서의 국립중앙도서관 출판시도서목록(CIP)은 서지정보유통지원시스템 홈페이지(http://seoji.nl.go.kr)와 국가자료공동목록시스템(http://www.nl.go.kr/kolisnet)에서 이용하실 수 있습니다.
(CIP제어번호 : CIP2013006925)

Semiosis of African American Religion
Its Symbols and Meanings Since Slavery

First printed May 20, 2013
First published May 30, 2013
Author Ahn, Mikyung
Publisher Park, Chul
Hankuk University of Foreign Studies Press Center
107 Imun-ro Dongdaemun-gu, Seoul 130-791, Korea
Tel: 82-2-2173-2495~7
Fax: 82-2-2173-3363
Homepage: http://press.hufs.ac.kr
e-mail: press@hufs.ac.kr
Registration of publisher: 6-6(Apr. 30, 1969)

ISBN 978-89-7464-837-4 94170 ₩18,000
ISBN 978-89-7464-832-9 94080 (set)

This work was supported by the National Research Foundation of Korea Grant funded by the Korean Government (NRF-2010-361-A00013).

There is neither Jew nor Greek, there is neither slave nor free, there is neither male nor female; for ye are all one in Christ Jesus.

(GALATIANS 3: 28)

Contents

Preface

Franklin Frazier argued that slavery was so devastating in America that it destroyed all African elements among black Americans; African-Americans lost all their African culture and tradition while undergoing slavery; they were in a stated of cultural limbo. African Americans have culture; especially black religious institutions have been the foundation of African American culture. Black church has been "an agency of social control, a sponsor of education, and a refuge in a hostile white world," and it has played a central role in African American life (Raboteau, 1980, p. X).

Nevertheless, the black church was a subject largely neglected or evaded by many scholars of religion or culture in America, not to mention in Korea. Therefore, there has been little work on black religion. This book will help understand the origin, the role, the symbols and meanings of the important subject, African-American religion by investigating slave narratives, black autobiographies, spirituals and the narratives of their religious experiences during slavery and after emancipation.

Moreover, religion is a process of on-going semiotic construction and displacement in which interpreters select paradigmatic elements to form syntagmatic combinations. In accordance with Peirce's triadic semiotics, Firstness in the African American religion has to do with the reality which African American people have faced since slavery, and the feeling which they have had in confronting their adversity. Secondness in black religion is associated with African Americans' reaction to their harsh reality and their way to overcome their agony. Thirdness in African American religion is related to their recognition, thoughts and self-consciousness of their reality or difficulties. This book will display the dynamic phenomena of African American religion, that is, semiosis of African American religion under Peirce's way of interpreting the world and religion.

This book owes much to discussion with my colleagues, Hyug Ahn, Byong-Chang Kang, Eunjeong Kim, Kyung-Nan Koh, Jong-Seok Soh, Jun Rae Cho, Soyeon Eom, Junhyun Kim, Yunhee Lee in Semiosis Research Center of Hankuk University of Foreign Studies. A number of other people have contributed to this book in some way or other. My thanks are due in particular to Paig-Ki Kim, Ki Sun Chun, Wonhoi Kim, DaeGeun Lim, Jae Hyup Lee, Sangmi Park, and Frank Concilus. I also wish to thank Noorey Kim, NoJin Chung, Changmin Jeon, Juwon Oh, and Sukha Shin.

Semiosis of Research Center, HUFS
May 2013

M.K.A

01

Introduction

Religion is a process of on-going semiotic construction and displacement in which interpreters select paradigmatic elements to form syntagmatic combinations. This religious semiosis has a tendency to take the form of conflicts. Religious symbols generally help us interpret some experiences or reality meaningfully, and they are supposed to be transformative. Religious symbols also help save people, shape communities, and tell the truth about what they represent, and affect spreading the value of religious realities (Neville, 2006; Shults, 2010).

Peirce played a crucial role in a philosophical shift toward highlighting the category of relationality in ontology and epistemology, claiming that all phenomena present a mixture of freedom and constraint. Since all things are inter-connected, signification does not lie in mental processes but an intrinsic dynamic of reality. Peirce also did not distinguish between substance and accidents which had made many epistemological proposals in western philosophy (Peirce, 1998, pp. 1-3). His classes of relations were triadic: Firstness, Secondness and Thirdness, and the categories were intrinsically interwoven and dynamically mediated. Firstness has to do with an immediate quality of feeling such as a feeling of pain, or a sense of redness, that compels our attention. Secondness is associated with the element of reaction in a phenomenon, and is the idea of the compulsiveness or hardness of experience. This is related to how we typically experience the world. Thirdness is explicitly linked to thought and self-consciousness (Peirce, 1998, p.160).

Peirce also highlighted the triadic relation between sign-object-interpretant. "A sign or representamen is a First which stands in such a genuine triadic relation to a Second, called its object, as to be capable of determining a Third, called its Interpretant to assume the same triadic relation to its Object in which it stands itself to the same Object." He further asserts that signs including symbols are not merely intelligible but as real as all other phenomenon in their dynamic continuity. In other words, signs are not always taken by interpreters to refer to objects in the same way. What makes a sign iconic, indexical or symbolic is not inherent in the sign itself but in the interpretation, that is, in the way that sign and object are interpreted in relation (Peirce, 1998, pp. 272-274).

In accordance with Peirce's triadic semiotics, Firstness in the African American religion has to do with the reality which African American people have faced since slavery, and the feeling which they have had in confronting their adversity. Secondness in black religion is associated with African Americans' reaction to their harsh reality and their way to overcome their agony. Thirdness in African American religion is related to their recognition, thoughts and self-consiousness of their reality or difficulties. Given Peirce's triadic semiotics, the meanings and symbols of African American religion can differ depending on who is its interpreter, for instance either slave holders or slaves, or either man or woman etc. This study will investigate the dynamic phenomena of African American religion, that is, semiosis of African American religion under Peirce's way of interpreting the world and religion.

Franklin Frazier argued that "Slavery was so devastating in America that it destroyed all African elements among black Americans." Some other whites also asserted that African-Americans lost all their African culture and tradition while undergoing slavery, and they were in a stated of cultural limbo. The argument that blacks have no culture is not different from Japanese contention under colonial period that Koreans are savage, and need protection. African Americans have culture; especially black religious institutions have been the foundation of African American culture. "An agency of social control, a sponsor of education, and a refuge in a hostile white world, "the black church has played a central role in African American life (Raboteau, 1980, p. X).

Nevertheless, the black church was a subject largely neglected or evaded by many scholars of religion or culture in America, not to mention in Korea. Therefore, there has been little work on black religion. This study aims at helping understand the origin, the role, the symbols and meanings of the important subject, African-American religion by investigating slave narratives, black autobiographies, spirituals and the story of their religious experiences during slavery and after emancipation.

During the revivals of the eighteenth and nineteenth centuries, many African Americans accepted Christianity and this has posed many troubling questions: How could black slaves adopt Christianity which was used by many whites to justify slavery?; How did the evangelization and conversion of African slaves to Christianity take place; what were main factors of the increase in conversation?; How could blacks love and believe in Christian God while they suffered under slavery?; How could Christianity were meaningful for blacks if it were a "White man's religion"? If the religion to which the slave converted was not same to the white man's Christianity, what was distinctive about African-American religion? These are the general questions that I have attempted to answer.

African Americans have had a long tradition of social and

political activism, and they also have had a long and deep tradition of religiosity (Mattis, 2001). African American religion has provided coherence to social and political life by providing blacks with common symbols, a shared collective identity, and systems of meaning and morality that manifest as a shared world view. In this regard, this study will explore how religion and its associated system of meanings and symbols have formed African American political life.

This study also investigates the complex and dynamic characteristics of contemporary African American religion: i) in terms of the relationship between gender and religion, especially the relationships between gender, race, poverty, and religious authority within the Black church; ii) in relation to contemporary African-American congregational worship practices-ecstatic, participatory worship distinctive to African-American congregations; iii) in terms of the relationship between religion and race for African Americans in this multiracial congregation; iv) regarding the growth of mega-churches and the role of charismatic leadership in the African American church.

Spirituality has always been significant concept to understand African American family life. The study of this concept will be helpful in understanding how African American families have historically used their belief in God to overcome the adversities they have confronted. Finally, this study investigates the symbols and meanings of these two key cultural components, food and religion by starting with a historical perspective on the role of food in a religious and cultural context.

02

World of Signs and Religion

1. Religious symbols

Religious symbols have both an interpretative and a practical function. Religious symbols generally help us interpret some experiences or reality meaningfully, and they are supposed to be transformative. It is considered that religious symbols are used to facilitate the transformation of personal, social or cultural character. More specifically, religious symbols affect intense transformations such as salvation, enlightenment, or basic attunement. Religious symbols are also dynamic in involving both the ongoing transformation of persons as well as semiotic codes (Neville, 1996, 2006). Peirce's triadic semiotics proposes that the pragmatic act of taking a sign to refer to an object is a constitutive element of interpretation. This means that questions about the meaning, reference, and even truth of an interpretation cannot be separated from the interpreter's actual purposive engagement in context (Shults, 2010, p. 717).

The distinctive human mode of engagement is the synthetic activity of imagination: Humans have the capacity to experience the world through images and the imagination integrates stimuli so that reality can be experienced as a world. The interpretation of religious symbols is not purely mental in that even the most abstract reflection is implicated in interpretive networks which engage the interpreter's environment (Neville, 2006, p. 31). If imagination plays a role in constructing the experiential world, it can be religious because it involves engagement with what interpreters take as ultimate boundary conditions for experience itself. Hence, it can be assumed that Religion is a natural and existential feature of human imaginative engagement (Neville, 1981, 1996, 2006).

One principle function of religious symbols, including doctrines, is to engage people with religious realities. What makes religious engagement distinctive is that it is intended as a response to a transformative power derived from a presumed ultimate source. All religious interpretations do not engage interpreters with this transformative power. In this regard, there is a distinction between the extensional structure of the semiotic code, which is relatively stable, and the intentional interpretation that treats the symbols as tools for engagement. The meaning of religious symbols can be understood only when we take into account the concrete, existential, and intentional context of the interpretation (Neville, 2006; Shults, 2010).

Religious symbols have double referents: Their primary reference is to the boundary conditions contrasting the finite and the infinite; their secondary reference is to the character or shape of the interpreters in their particular context individually or communally. Both are integrated in his understanding of what religious symbols do and how they are both transformed and transforming. Diverse cultures have developed various symbols and symbolic networks for indicating the ultimate boundary conditions of worldliness (Neville, 1996, 2006). Religious symbols are also intended to refer to "that which is not wholly finite, which transcends determinate identity" (Neville 1996, p. 58). The real object is not simply a finite thing of world-constructing importance but the finite thing in contrast with the infinite. Therefore, symbols are considered finite signs taken by finite interpreters to refer to finite objects in some finite respect. Symbols are determinate and determining. The infinite is that which is essentially indeterminate and there cannot exist finite terms to determine it (Neville, 1996, 2006; Shults, 2010).

In Neville's adaptation of his pragmatic semiotic metaphysics, what is meaningful is not the Peircean way of understanding truth, but the way of carryover of value from the object to the interpreter in some respect. The interpretive acts are a real engagement with the divine mediated through religious symbols. If we accept Peirce's model of triadic nature of semiotic engagement, understanding of religious symbols should not be limited to analysis of the extensional code of signs such as doctrines or even to the relation of those signs to objects in the world (Shults, 2010, p. 721).

Because symbols operate within concrete intentional interpretations, they also represent the effective difference that is made in the practical experience of the interpreter through the symbolic engagement. The meaning of a religious symbol is determined by both its reference to an extensional semiotic code and its reference to the intentional context of the interpreter. This reference to the internal and intentional context cannot be ignored because it is necessary to the act of interpretation and constitutes the effective meaning of the symbol. Representations of cognitive signs are "habits of construing things in a certain way so as to shape human enjoyments, responses, purposes and actions" (Shults, 2010, p. 723).

In a communal context, the symbol may function to organize the lives of those who experience the divine as a secure and protective presence. The way in which the symbols function will be shaped by the particular state or developmental stage of the religious devotee. In devotional contexts, a religious symbol is employed not only to address and engage the devotee's soul but also to engage the divine. Symbols may need to evoke sometimes terror or comfort, in order to influence transformation of the soul in relation to the divine. In this context, religious symbols are supposed to help save people, shape communities, and tell the truth about what they represent. Religious symbols also influence the carryover of the value of religious realities, which are ultimately related to some finite/infinite contrast and to the interpreter in his or her particular context. In so doing, religious symbols transform people and are transformed by people (Neville, 1996, 2006; Shults, 2010).

2. Peirce's triadic semiotics

Peirce played a significant role in a philosophical shift toward highlighting the category of relationality in ontology and epistemology. He did not begin with the assumptions of substance metaphysics involving: dualism (all is divided into two kinds of substance) or monism (all is one kind of substance, material or ideal). Regarding the relational inter-connection of all things, Pierce proposed an alternative he called *synechism*, the tendency to regard everything as continuous (from the Greek syneches, meaning continuous). The synechist believes and asserts that all phenomena are of one character. Peirce does not accept a quantative separation between material and immaterial things, and claims that all phenomena present a mixture of freedom and constraint. If all things are inter-connected, signification does not lie in mental processes but an intrinsic dynamic of reality. In this regard, Peirce's approach could play an important role in the one-moment of religion and science (Peirce, 1998, pp. 1-3).

Peirce also resisted the basic distinction between substance and accidents which had structured so many epistemological proposals in western philosophy. His classes of relations were triadic: Firstness, Secondness and Thirdness. Peirce always claimed that categories were intrinsically interwoven and dynamically mediated, reflecting his metaphysical synechism. In one of his definitions he writes: "Firstness is that which is such as it is positively and regardless of anything else. Secondness is that which is as it is in a second something's being as it is, regardless of any third. Thirdness is that whose being consists in its bringing about a secondness." For Peirce, these interdependent categories are really continuous, mutually mediated in all ideational and pragmatic engagement (Peirce, 1998, p. 267).

Firstness has to do with an immediate quality of feeling, of the suchness of a phenomenon. It is the idea of an impression such as a feeling of pain, or a sense of redness, that compels our attention. Secondness is associated with the element of reaction in a phenomenon. It is the idea of the compulsiveness or hardness of experience, that which is as it is as over-against or other to some First. This is how we typically experience the world whether as agents or patients or not. Thirdness is explicitly linked to thought and self-consciousness for Peirce. As he explains elsewhere, "the Third is the idea of that which is such as it is as being a Third or medium between a Second and its First. That is to say, it is a Representation as an element of the phenomenon." Peirce also used these triadic categories to develop a new classification of the sciences but it is sufficient to note that his triadic epistemology involve and include his holistic, dynamic and pragmatic (non-dualist) understanding of symbolic engagement (Peirce, 1998, p. 160).

In other words, Peirce's argument for the complex ways in which sign may be taken or engaged by interpreters is embedded within his commitment to metaphysical synechism and triadic theory of knowledge. Avoiding a simple dualism between sign and object, Peirce stressed the triadic relation between sign-object-interpretant. "A sign or representamen is a First which stands in such a genuine triadic relation to a Second, called its object, as to be capable of determining a Third, called its Interpretant to assume the same triadic relation to its Object in which it stands itself to the same Object." Perice is careful to emphasize that this cannot be reduced to dyadic semiotic relations or even to a complex of such dyadic relations. The mediating triadic relationality of signification is genuine and irreducible. Moreover, signs including symbols are intelligible or ideational but real like all other phenomenon in their dynamic continuity (Peirce, 1998, p. 272).

This is in the same line with Peircean semiotics: signs are not always taken by interpreters to refer to objects in the same way. His treatment of the pragmatic models of engaging a signified object, of the rendering of interpretants is also trichotomous: representamen can be an icon, an index, or a symbol. In other words, we might say that a sign can represent an object mimetically, indicatively, or conventionally. An icon is "a representamen whose representative quality is a Firstness of it as a First". This kind of interpretant takes the sign mimetically as involving resemblance or similarity to the object in some sense (Peirce, 1998, pp. 273-274).

A portrait, for example, resembles the object it intends to signify. An index is a "representamen whose representative character consists in its being an individual Second." Such interpretants signify some kind of temporal, physical, causal or otherwise indicative relation to the object. For example, a weathervane indicates the direction of the wind, or a smell or noise indicates an animal's readiness to mate. A symbol is a "representamen whose representative character consists precisely in its being a rule that will determine its Interpretant." Peirce implies that a symbol is a law or regularity of the indefinite future, but a law necessarily governs or is embodied in individuals and prescribes some of their qualities, which means icons and indexes can be constituents of symbols. Peirce uses examples from language, for instance combinations of sounds form words, which symbolize meanings or ideas, as well as from cultural practices, for example, a wedding ring as a symbol of marriage in some societies. It is important to note that what makes a sign iconic, indexical or symbolic is not inherent in the sign itself but in the interpretation, in other words, in the way in which sign and object are regarded or considered in relation (Peirce, 1998, p. 274).

Peirce's triadic semiotics is attractive to many contemporary interpreters of religion because it provides a way of explaining how religious symbols function in the pragmatic, spatio-temporal, social and cosmic engagement of persons in particular cultures. Symbols are not only abstract ideas that must be somehow connected to the material world but also they are continuously interwoven in all human engagement, dynamically entangled as a causal force in social life. While symbols mediate future possibilities icons and indexes belong to past and present experience, respectively. This open, relational, dynamic and pragmatic approach to understanding human symbolic functioning has been met with enthusiasm across a variety of disciplines concerned with understanding and explaining human culture-including religion (Peirce, 1998).

In this context, however, it makes sense to limit ourselves to a few examples of the appropriation of Peircean semiotics in disciplines which are more directly concerned with the way in which human symbolic capacity plays a role in cultural and religious questions of ultimate meaning like "why are we here?" Peircean semiotic metaphysics is inherently pragmatic, which implies that for serious appropriation of his work, one should inquire into the appropriateness of our conceptual linking of Christian symbols and explore the extent to which our practical engagement with reality through such symbols is appropriately transformative (Mircea, 1961a; Shults, 2010).

Their argument is based on the intriguing parallels between Perice's three classes of relations or categories-firstness, secondness, and thirdness-and three persons of the Trinity-father, son, and Holy spirit. Symbols are always taken in actual contexts of real interpretation (Shults, 2010, p. 726). The use of the symbols *father* and *son*, for example, is taken differently in various contexts and by different interpreters. They played a special role in the network of meaning that characterized the patriarchal culture of the patristic period. Their function in contemporary culture has been criticized by many feminists. The key question is how these male symbols function in context. We can imagine devotional contexts in which they still can mediate spiritual formation, and cultic contexts in which they still may shape communities in ways that valuably relate human life to the divine. In an academic theological context, however, it is important to emphasize that these symbols also break on the infinite and to acknowledge that for many they are not only broken but dead. Success in this venture may require Pericean semiotic metaphysics to accept that Christian symbols are not static but dynamic. The meaning of symbols is always being changed in each and every intentional engagement with the extensional semiotic code. Peirce's pragmatism may have significant effect on the transformation of Christian symbols (Peirce 1998, Shults, 2010, p. 727).

The doctrinal symbol of incarnation, which emerged and was shaped in relation to Trinitarian symbols, also has to do with the human encounter with the infinite. The symbols of Jesus relate him to God as the founding finite /infinite contrast for Christians. The task of Christology traditionally has been considered explaining how the infinite divine word became finite human flesh (Neville, 2006). Peircean categories, especially his taxonomy of signs, offer a potentially fruitful way of reframing Christological questions and symbolic formulations (Robinson & Southgate, 2010).

The particular quality that is god's presence was there in Jesus, leaving it unclear whether that quality could also be embodied in other signs or how that quality can be present here and now for us. As Peirce insists, signs are not static entities and they are always being taken, being dynamically engaged and corrected through ongoing pragmatic interaction. Persons might take the sign of Jesus' life as much of the traditional imagery surrounding the incarnation, such as iconically, indexically or symbolically or all at once referring to the transformative divine presence (Neville, 2006; Robinson & Southgate, 2010).

Much of the traditional imagery surrounding the incarnation such as the virgin birth of a holy child in a stable or the descent of the Son of God from heaven, may have its place in the devotional and even communal contexts of some Christians. However, in the context of academic theology, and especially in the context of interdisciplinary dialogue with contemporary biology and cosmology, taking such symbols representationally is implausible (Orange, 1984; Shults, 2010, p. 729).

In such dialogues theology should be clear about its own task, which includes attending to the dynamics of human attempts to engage ultimate reality (the infinite, the divine, God, nothingness, and so forth) in ways that are transformative. Using Peirce's terminology, we may say that "theology's First is the impression of limitation itself, the sense of being finite; The existential reaction of this ultimate being-limited comprises theology's Second; Considerations of such Firsts as Seconds are theology's Thirds: religious symbols that have brought about interpretations through which persons engage their object considered not as one finite thing among many but as that which grounds the contingency conditions of all finite things." Theological imagination cannot escape its limitation through the infinite because the infinite is not a determinate reality but is what ultimately grounds all finite considerations (Orange, 1984; Shults, 2010, p. 730).

In our context, especially for African American religion, as seen above, Peirce also proposed an important resource for developing new ways of thinking, or new ways of interpreting interpretation. Based on Pericean semiotic metaphysics and Peirce's pragmatism, in this study, we will investigate the conceptual linking of African American religious symbols with the reality and study the extent to which our practical engagement with reality through such symbols is appropriately transformative. In addition, we will explore how black Christian symbols have been dynamic.

3. Nevilles' religious symbolism

Neville (1996, 2006) claims that symbolism, religion and imagination are closely associated. He understands imagination as the capacity to experience things with images. Imagination is the elementary kind of causal process in human beings that gives rise to experience integrated with the forms of experiential worldliness. Imagination and religion are intimately connected. In the experienced world, something appears as shaping the world as such. These are paradigmatic orienting appearances that have symbolic value for defining ultimate shape (Neville, 1996).

Imagination is always religious in that imagination deals

with the very conditions for the construction of the world in function of synthetic world-making. Neville (1996) argues that imagination cannot frame its experiential elements in a human way without the orienting importance of pervasively or seasonally appearing images that function as boundary conditions for worldliness. The phenomenon of religion is the cultural phenomenon of inducing symbols of the boundary conditions.

Religious symbols are not the common kind with which one can interact to clarify and improve one's signs and interpretive habits. The logical objects referred to by religious symbols are finite in the ordinary sense. Religious symbols are those that refer to borderline or world-making things, that is to say, those that form the very worldliness of the world. Although various cultures and theologies construe this difference- making object differently for instance, as a creator, gods, or sheer nothingness, they all refer to what stands between the finiteness of the structured world and the infinite (Neville, 1996, 2006).

Neville (1996, p. 58) proposes the use of the phrase "finite / infinite contrast" as a technical term for the primary referent of religious symbols. He calls this referent the divine because these symbols mark what is experienced as a special condition defining worldliness or world construction. Although the term "infinite" is commonly associated with theism, he believes it can be used philosophically to indicate what defines conditions or determines the contingency of the cosmos itself, which provides the possibility of the experience of worldliness. This allows him to find "finite/infinite" contrasts in all religious symbolic engagement. Since this capacity is ingredient to human imagination, Neville (2006, p. 65) insists that it is not restricted to understanding the boundary conditions of the world offered by organized religions. He observes that Stephen Hawking's hypothesis about a grand unified theory of the universe is itself an image for the "finite / infinite" contrast in respect of the world's existence.

What makes the explicitly religious form of imaginative synthesis unique is that symbols break on the infinite (See Neville, 2006; Peirce, 1998). Symbols do not work on finite/infinite contrasts the way they do in the engagement of finite things. This means that only broken symbols can truly refer to such boundary-constructing or world-making conditions. The main point is that this emphasis on the brokenness of religious symbols allows Neville to accept a humble negative theology, which says that we cannot refer to God in conceptual language, while also arguing that religious symbols can truly engage reality, precisely at the imaginative limiting of finite/infinite contrasts (see Neville, 1996, 2006; Peirce, 1998).

This approach is inextricably linked to Neville's emphasis on the importance of tending to the context of an interpretation. Here is where Peirce's approach is particularly helpful: one must tend to the different ways in which signs are taken iconically, indexically or symbolically by religious persons to refer to divine objects in particular context. Neville (1996) distinguishes between extensional and intensional interpretations as one way of clarifying what it means to take symbols in extensional and intentional interpretations. The possible interpretations within or the potential meanings extended throughout the explicit code of a semiotic system are its extensional interpretation. The primary meaning of interpretation, however, is an intentional act of actually interpreting something for which the semiotic code contains possible forms. In other words, an intentional interpretation has existential location, and uses signs to engage real, intentional referents. Such interpretations consist in the impact to the symbols '"finite/infinite" contrasts on the experience of the interpreter or interpreting community as mediated by the symbol. In this context, this impact is the symbol's content meaning integrated into practice (Neville, 1996, pp. 115-119; See Peirce, 1998).

Moreover, the context of an interpretant cannot be abstracted from the actual dynamic, causal processes of ongoing pragmatic engagement of particular interpreters. For Neville, this means that whether or not a religious symbol truly engages depends not only on the context but also on the developmental stage and transformational concerns of the person imaginatively intending the finite/infinite contrast. The symbol of god walking in the garden of Eden, for example, may be taken iconically, indexically, or symbolically; furthermore, it might be taken or intended differently in various domains such as what Neville calls public, ordinary, ad devotional life. This requires pastoral sensitivity and attention to the way in which symbolic engagement transforms persons. Neville observes that human beings have the capacity to respond to the ultimately orienting conditions for existence as such. He argues that the task of theology is not only to reflect on ultimate matters of value such as finite/infinite contrasts but also promote the living of lives informed by what is ultimately important to guide human comportment in the face of ultimacy (Neville, 2006, pp. 202-203).

4. Interpretation of Sacred Literature

Throughout its history, the study of religion has explored the notion of origin and stories of origins, primordial or historical, religious or scholarly, factual or legendary (see Eliade, 1959, 1969; Masuzawa, 1993). Scholars of religion have searched repeatedly for some fundamental explanations of "the totality of a phenomenon, its meaning, its raison detre, or its place within a system of purposes or functions, in the stories religions tell of its coming-to be or in the scholar's analysis of its coming-to be" (Evola, 2005, p. 48).

In larger formations of myths or religions, creation stories, a response to a religious symbol or a divinity look alike. From a semiotic point of view, the situation of the origin, again of any particular cultural or religious datum, is precisely analogous to that of genres as described by Tzvetan Todorov: Religions originate by transforming, combining or even inverting pre-existing cultural materials. Syncretistic religion is a redundant term. The religion constitutes variations upon pre-existing materials (Evola, 2005, pp. 50-51; Smith, 1982).

In this respect, the primary source for the study of religion is this body of preexistent material. The question of origin is used to ask the conditions which brought about acts of transformation, dissemination, incorporation, contestation, or preservation of this pre-existent material. In this reformation of the origination of religious materials, the questions that a theory of religion must ask are the following: "what is the nature of this pre-existent material?; What are its internal relations?; How does it retain some sense of continuous identity over time and place yet undergo constant change; What occasions specific instances of its evocation, its application, its transformation?" (Corrinton, 1987a; Evola, 2005, p. 51).

The nature of the pre-existent material is that of an ensemble of signifiers. In other words, religion is essentially semiotic. The internal relations of this ensemble of signifiers can be best understood by the structuralist concepts of *langue et parole*, language as a system and language as an act of articulation, or as the relation between a paradigmatic axis and a syntagmatic axis (Hawkes, 1977, pp. 19-22; Evola, 2005, p. 52).

The continuous identity of a religion as well as its on-going permutations is products of acts of interpretation. Jonathan Z. Smith (1982) captures all three elements in his description of sacred persistence as a product of the relationship between a canon and a hermeneute. The believer as hermeneute is associated with the structured ensemble of signifiers, or canon, as a reader has to do with a text. The canon itself is the definer of the parameters of interpretation as well as the product of interpretation. Subsequent interpretations stay within the bounds of the received tradition or claim to find the real meaning in the canon, which starts from the received interpretations (Corrington, 1987a; Evola, 2005, p. 52; Smith, 1982).

The perennial feature of the sign which can explain all the instances of its iteration is comprehended and accepted in a broad, semiotic sense. Whether hidden or manifest, whether conscious or unconscious, all religious discourse is so striated and saturated by and with the speech of the other. In other words, it is a key element in a semiotic theory of religion that the semiotician of religion must define it as "the constitutive other" (Evola, 2005, p. 52; Robinson, 2004).

It is an appropriate aspiration of a theory to aim at an all-embracing account of its delineated field of phenomena.

The ubiquity of symbolic behavior, or " the sheer semioticity of the world" (Holquist 1990, p. 49), suggests that a semiotic theory meets a chance at such scope. Whether it forms an all-embracing theory or not, what is clear is that such a theoretical framework is very useful for the elucidation of the textual practices of both religionists and scholars of religion. As *langue* is to *parole*, specific texts manifest an historical discourse, or many historical discourses to a greater or lesser degree. The semiotician's job is to delineate the common, inter-textual discourses with historical and linguistic specificity. Once the diachronic exegesis of a discourse, or a braid of discourses is delimited, the semiotician must analyze the internal structure of each particular braid of discourse. Finally the semiotician must trace out the effects of the movement of an object of discourse between specific, bounded discursive formations. The semioticians also should make an a priori assumption neither of continuity not of complete difference, but analyze the specific structuring events in each movement and the specific effects of specific discourses (Evola, 2005, p. 63; Robinson, 2004; Robinson & Southgate, 2010).

The description of the relation between a canon of signs and an interpretive language in the canon, and the description of that relationship in a third text repeat precisely the same structural relationship. In this context, the situation between object-language and meta-language, between interpreter and interpreter of interpretation, is the same as James Clifford has said of the text of ethnography: "A scientific ethnography normally establishes a privileged allegorical register it identifies as theory, interpretation, or explanation" (Clifford, 1986, p. 103). However, once all meaningful levels in a text, including theories and interpretations are recognized as allegorical, it becomes difficult to view one of them as privileged, accounting for the rest (Clifford, 1986; Evola, 2005).

Thus, the ways of interpretating and understanding a religious symbol look similar in various sacred texts. Religion is originated by transforming, combining or even inverting pre-existing cultural materials. In other words, religion comprises variations upon pre-existing materials. In this regard, it will also be meaningful to investigate the preexistent material as the key source for the study of religion, especially the African American religion.

5. Corrington's world semiosis and the evolution of meaning

The structures of world semiosis are the most pervasive in the various universes available to human probing. The concept of world to be used here refers somewhat elliptically to any and all worlds or universes that are or could be encountered in any way. Further, the concept of world refers to any worldly structure that may forever be beyond the reach of sign-using organisms like ourselves. The concept of "worldhood (weltheit)" as partially developed by Heidegger, refers to the sheer availability of worlds to the human process on the most genetic level (Corrington, 1988, 1994, 2000, pp. 168-169).

Similarly to Peirce (1998) and Neville (2006), Corrinton (2000) also claims that meaning is not a static structure and is subject to its own forms of evolution, both in terms of its emergence and its unfolding within particular orders in a particular respects. On the deepest levels, the evolution of meanings is correlated to the betweenness structures which include the spirit of interpretation within certain rare and fragile orders of interaction. The dialectic of plenitude and emptiness permeates all semiotic worlds, and serves to sustain their innumerable unfolding and mysteries. The meanings encountered in sacred folds represent the most intense and evolved of the meanings available to the human process. World semiosis cannot be described outside of the context of the evolution of meaning (Corrington, 1988, 1994, 2000).

5.1 The sign /object correlation

The current philosophical climate did not identify the depth-structure of the sign/object relation, primarily because of a commitment to a semiotic idealism that gives signs too much freedom from those objects with which they are interpreted. When Peirce's seemingly innocent tri-semiotic theory is grafted onto the first dyad of sign and object, it can be said to be almost overwhelmingly ideal. Interpretants can exist because of human forms of semiosis that can manipulate signs without probing into their underlying objective correlates. Peirce provides convergent lines that will eventually allow the object to appear fully through its interpretants (Corrington, 1994, 2000).

As shown in section 2.2, however, Peirce still privileges human forms of mentality, and most of his followers have neglected the potential naturalistic and ecstatic dimension of his perspective in order to highlight the manipulative and allegedly postmodern aspects of semiosis. Peirce can be criticized for it and even his post-Kantian elements still remain strongly within the Kant of the Schema:

> The schema is in itself always only a product of the imagination; but since the synthesis of the latter has as its aim no individual intuition but rather only the unity in the determination of sensibility, the schema is to be distinguished from an image. Thus, if I place five points in a row… this is an image of the number five. On the contrary, if I only think a number in general, which could be five or a hundred, this thinking is more the representation of a method for representing a multitude (e.g., a thousand) in accordance with a certain concept than the image itself, which in this case I could survey and compare with the concept only with difficulty. Now this representation of a general procedure of the imagination for providing a concept

> with its image is what I call the schema for this concept (Kant, 1781, p. A140).

Kant's system caused him to stay within the circle of his transcendent subject by connecting a bare singular image with an equally bare concept through the mysterious realm of the pure image as woven together by the unconscious schema. The schema functions as a kind of a temporal interpretant that makes objectness possible through internal semiosis. The schema is temporal but it is based on the pretemporal. Therefore, it is not subject to semiotic entropy, that is to say, a feature of most forms of semiotic idealism. Heidegger tried to reject the temporal dimension of Kant's schematism, but tried to impose his own categorical delineations on the problematic (Heidegger, 1929, 1973). Peirce's perceptual judgment that applied a predicate to a percept is a more temporal, which is closer to Heidegger's version of Kant. The perceptual judgment as an evolutionary dimension at least makes a form of semiotic naturalism possible. Nevertheless, this process is still biased toward the schema/perceptual judgment, and is distant from the manifold to which it is applied. Clearly, Peirce's percept is more self-shaping than Kant's chaotic manifold, but it is still held in an "eschatological domain where it will only carry proper meaning at the end of thermodynamic time" (Corrington, 1988, 1993a, 1995, 2000, p. 171).

The term "object" is limited in scope and only retains its

use in the current perspective for it functions continuously in both pragmaticist and phenomenological perspectives. It is a short-hand designation for the far more flexible and generic designation "orders of relevance". The term "object" should not be confined to any spatial or container connotations. Anything can be an object in this special sense, whether a thought, a possibility, a desire, a probability or a law-like habit of nature. When the term "object" is given this great interpretive license, the only domain where it is not allowed to trespass is not aware of nature, which is not an order of relevance in any sense (Corrington, 1988, 1995, 2000, p. 172).

There are two insights here: "i) that the object is always more, in some sense, than any and all signs that make it available either to other objects or to specific sign users, and ii) that the object has a sphere of dominance of resistance that is both semiotic and pre-and postsemiotic." Object is presemiotic as long as it contains traits that are not translatable into a sign in some respect whereas object is postsemiotic as far as it is formed by betweenness structures and momenta that are more primitive than the prospective. The object, that is, "order of relevance" clearly has semiotic traits in that it is, whether weakly or strongly, relevant to another order of relevance. In other words, these signs need to be interpreted by another mind. The concept of sign is retained to entail that of sign interpreter. The interpreter is usually considered human, even though many semioticians are now willing to talk about forms of biosemiotics. However, "what of those sign/object relations that are not organic, and that might be merely causal? Is there only an object/object relation, or is there a concept of the virtually semiotic made a brief appearance as one entrance point to this problematic?" (Corrington, 1995, 2000, p. 173). Deely (1990) investigated the nexus where physical causality develops into semiotic causality all prior to any sense of final causality:

> Before there are actually signs, there are signs virtually that is there are beings and events so determined by other beings and events that, in their own activity as so determined, they determine yet further series of beings and events in such a way that the last terms in the series represent the first terms by the mediation of the middle terms. (Deely, 1990, p. 87)

The time process is semiotic, even when so-called physical objects are involved. Any present state of a physical order of relevance will contain signs of its previous states, whether decoded by humans or not. Josiah Royce claimed that the entire time process was one involving a series of signs commenting on previous signs. For instance, in looking at the face of the Grand Canyon, it is clear that each stratum contains its own semiotic "commentary" on its own and its antecedents' histories (Corrington, 1995, 2000, p. 173).

There are concrescences of past states that have become hardened and obtained in the present. At the same time, the object will also have more recent traits that could only be what they are because of the antecedent traits. The Grand Canyon does not need human or other interpreters to be a sign of itself and its past. It is its sum of signs no matter what form of consciousness may or may not interact with it. Hence, in the prehuman order, the sign/object relation is so intimate that there may be no way of making the distinction that is so pertinent for the sign-using self. The current perspective affirms that even physical orders of relevance, the seemingly most distanced from semiosis, are actually semiotic (Corrington, 1988, 1994, 1995, 2000).

The object is fully semiotic in that it already is its signs of its past states assuming that it occupies the thermodynamic arrow of time. However, there are traits which may not be semiotic, and may not be available within the object. The object will be its signs of itself, but will also participate in the presemiotic in ways that are beyond the reach of interpreters and the object itself without the object being personified. In other words, the object is not completely exhausted by its actual semiotic traits, or its virtual forms of semiosis, but it will also be the locus for those nonsemiotic traits that participate in the under conscious of nature. The object, whether physical or not, will be presemiotic, actually semiotic, and virtually semiotic only if it has potential semiotic traits that can be actualized by sign-using selves of whatever biological complexity (Corrington, 1990b).

For example, the Grand Canyon does not know that it is a sign of itself but it is in fact a sign. It is an anthropocentric prejudice that signs must be known to be such by a form of awareness that is fully intentional. A formal structural principle is a sign of itself whether discovered by sign users or not and its discovery may only disclose part of its complexity, hence making it as much virtual as actual. There is a progression from the more primitive form of sign as object or object as sign, to the separation of sign from object when some form of awareness makes the sign loose from its embeddedness in a causal history or structure. An order of relevance will be presemiotic if it participates in the underconscious of nature, and it will be actually semiotic as far as it is a sign of itself, and it has semiotic traits that can be further actualized by a sign-using self (Corrington, 1994, 2000).

In the semiotic cosmology of Sarte, he has a very different philosophical perspective, and his consciousness may be a strange and displaced decompression in the worlds of semiosis. Sarte thinks that the consciousness may generate more problems than it solves. If consciousness did not exist, the sign/object relationship would only be minimally problematic for other organic forms which have built-in evolutionary mechanisms for decoding and sign-translating. Once the reflexive turn occurs and subjectivity reaches out over the worlds of semiosis, objectness takes a new veil of semiosis that is further complicated by the projection and transference.

In the realm of psycho-semiosis an extreme hermeneutic pessimism can be avoided through the positive insights of a generically reconstructed psychoanalysis. This process makes it possible to sort through projections as any attempted semiotic cosmology (Corrington, 1984, 1988, 2000).

Husserl proposes that one of the basic acts of phenomenological description is the bracketing out of existence claims, that is, somewhat subjectivistic version of ontological parity. In an ordinal phenomenology, Husserl's project is completed for the commitment to parity more successfully by giving the phenomenon, not the subject. Its full reality is accomplished by rejecting any notion of degrees of being. The phenomenology practiced by ecstatic naturalism has a more radical decentering of consciousness than Husserl's and Heidegger's. Their consciousness remains within a process and the innumerable orders of nature natured. If consciousness is decentered, partially through the strenuous requirements of ontological parity, what access do sign users have to objects that helps us figure out the sign/object relation? (Corrington, 1992b, 1993a, 1994, 2000, p. 176)

The unconscious working in and through the interactive, i.e. transference and counter-transference field has its own intentionality and its own relation to orders of relevance. In other words, its own intentionality and relation to orders of relevance serve the principle of ontological parity without any conscious effort. The unconscious can function to bring priority driven consciousness back to its dimly sense understanding of parity. The goal of any phenomenological description is to explore the rhythms of the self-showing of the order of relevance with which it is bound so as to find the right measure of the sign/object correlation. Any order of relevance can be minimally a sign of itself. As the unconscious is a basis of projections, it is also a scanning system that has deep evolutionary reasons for getting the object right. The over-determined sphere of projection, with its species transference, has the positive role of enhancing the semiotic universe by holding open spaces for interpretation and the augmentation of traits. However, it is also a sphere with having its heat cooled by a counter-movement in which the object is gradually out of those projections that cover over its self-giving (Corrington, 1988, 1994, 2000).

Corrington (2000) takes an example that shows an unusual level of semiotic density in the human world, for instance, a large and perhaps religiously powerful tree that may be hundreds of years old. Structuralist semiology often uses this example in distinguishing between the sign and the signified. For delving into the sign and object relation, Corrington further assumes that the tree now functions within the ordinal location of certain neopagan practices that divinize it in terms of a sense of those immanent and earthly powers that have been rejected by the tree Western monotheisms. The tree can take mythic proportions as a symbol of the center of the world or as a symbol of regeneration on the edges of thermodynamic time. Then what exactly is the tree itself? This may be an absurd question as the tree is all of its ordinal locations, all of its ordinal options, and all of is spheres of relevance, whether it is known or not (Corrington, 1988, 1995, 2000).

This ancient tree is an object that has determined traits, and many of the traits were activated by the unconscious that we have ironically invoked to help us out of this dilemma of endless semiosis. We begin the movement toward the tree in itself-giving by making as many of our projections as self-conscious as possible. This is done through a series of rotations in which contrary traits are projected onto the tree. This is a form of resistance that is between the subject and the object, pushing contraries into the realm of internal conflict as housed in an external object. It is obvious to the sign-using self that there is now a semiotic overload and the distinction between the sign and its object becomes much sharper. For instance, we can contrast a molecular understanding with the neopagan one, or can distinguish an economic from an aesthetic ordinal location. A gap begins to open up with more and more clarity: the signs of the tree are not necessarily embedded in the tree in its own self-showing. This gap is a gift of the spirit that holds open the mobile space between human projection and its intentional objects. The gap resonates with a field of possible interpretations, but also keeps any given interpretation from collapsing back into the object. This is of course a limit condition under the condition of finitude, but phenomenological inquiry can enter into this momentum when it lets go of one projection after another (Corrington, 1988, 1990b, 1994, 2000).

Projections resist each other as long as they are contraries. However, this projection only takes place when thought persists that any given trait is the only one possible. An ordinal analysis can live with contraries given that each member of the contrast is understood to occupy its own order. Thus the tree can be considered being a molecular structure and the mythic center of my religious world if these traits allowed their own provenance in their respective orders. If this deeper insight takes place, each trait becomes less likely to collapse into the tree itself. Two insights have thus occurred into the sign/object correlation:"(1) there is a gap that holds open the space between projected traits and the object (a special kind of resistance that is a gift of the spirit and (2) incompatible traits can coexist if they are seen to occupy different orders, which further pries any given sign loose that limit its claims." (Corrington, 2000, p. 178).

Now let us take a look at semiotic minimalism that may seem to be in tension with the plentitude of the ordinal perspective. The ordinal perspective follows the innumerable ways in which an order of relevance will obtain in the world although there are often practical reasons for preferring one order to another. Under conditions of extreme need we may cut down the ancient tree to convert it into heat energy, or at the other extreme we may protect it with civil laws so that its unique traits are preserved. However, the tree is never reducible to any of its orders (Corrington, 1990b, 1994, 2000).

How does the tree show itself in this ordinal plenitude? The answer is obvious, although it may be profoundly difficult to enact in practice. On one level, the tree is fully self-showing when phenomenology has the rhythms of each of its available ordinal locations. This is the first step of self-showing, in which contraries can emerge as protected from each other by their ordinal locatedness. Phenomenology prefers the semiotic plentitude which is the mark of any object affecting the human process in any way. There is a depth-correlation between the self-showing of the order of relevance and the receptors in the unconscious that actively probe into the preprojective features of the object. There is an encounter with the object/object sign that underlies the sign/object relation in the more robust ordinal sense. This correlation does not bring us a more real object only one that is far less overburdened with semiotic noise. Thought is never compelled to privilege the full ordinal rotation (often filled with projection) over the simpler self-showing of the object through the unconscious, both because of energy constraints and because of the impulses coming from the object prior to its being clothed in projections (Corrington, 2000, pp. 179-180)

Let us take an example of how dream works. The unconscious was shown to have a compensatory relationship to consciousness. That is, whenever consciousness has a one-sided relationship both to itself and to its world, the unconscious will know how to balance the manic projections and distortions of consciousness. In other words, whenever consciousness has a one-sided relationship both to itself and to this world, the unconscious will know how to balance the manic projections and distortions of consciousness. This is logic as ancient as the rise of consciousness itself and one that has proven itself over and over again in the analytic context. In terms of the self-showing of the object, this is manifest in a counter-field of awareness that undercuts the projections that it has itself manifested through consciousness. (Corrington, 1988, 1990b, 2000, pp. 180-182)

Projections in general will always exist, but their specificity is almost always available to phenomenological probing. Hence the unconscious knows when it should project something overdetermined and when the projection has been recognized for what it is. The object is fully implicated in this process as its ordinal features are enhanced or diminished by the moment of the unconscious. Here the concept of resistance takes on another fold. The object will in some sense be known in its more primal self-showing by the unconscious. This is precisely why overdetermined projections emerged into and through consciousness, because of the gap between how consciousness sees the object and how the unconscious encounters it. It is as if the unconscious wants to propel consciousness into an absurd series of ordinal enrichments in order to force it to founder on its own folly. Thus the unconscious grants both manic plenitude and shipwreck, both ordinal fecundity and primal simplicity, all in service of the self-showing of the object (Corrington, 1988, 1990b, 1993a, 1994, 2000).

Semiotic space needs to be filled, but projections represent only one kind of sign material. Objects both resist and call forth projection, while the unconscious also both generates and overcomes projections in its continuing dialectic with consciousness. The priority here is to say that desire is the foundation for knowledge, while knowledge serves, for good or ill, the objects of desire. This thought is as old as Plato, but needs to be woven into a phenomenology signs and their objects so that the knowledge relation is allowed to play the role it must in the drama of the self-showing of objects. In the phenomenological transfiguration of desire into assimilative sensitivity, the object and the unconscious work more closely together to manifest their relevant traits to the sign-using self. From the standpoint of ecstatic naturalism, the object in itself is closer to us than Kant's numeral sphere, but differently available to us than Peirce's dynamic object, which exerts a rather primitive form of resistance. The withdrawal of projections is a product of the more subtle resistance emerging from the orders of relevance that surround the self in process. When the object comes to us in its most primitive form, it no longer wears a human face. The tree can show itself on the edges of language, putting great pressure on any form of linguistic contrivance that would render it into manifest structures (Corrington, 1988, 1990b, 1993a, 2000).

5.2 Spirits

This section examines how the current perspective uses the concept of spirit to understand the foundation of ethics and communal transformation? The spirit is not a person, not omnipotent, not omniscient, not omnipresent, not a body of signs ready to be decoded, and is not a reality that existed prior to the other orders of the world. Therefore, anything like the Christian notion of the immanent trinity is rejected. How does the spirit enter into the community of interpreters enabling some kind of moral transformation? In order to return to our example of the anti-racism campaign within the context of a congregational-style church, the spirit should do two things. First, it must open the members of the community to the realities that have made the community function in the first player. In other words, the spirit should let the members of the community confront the structures of racism that have given these members economic freedom and intellectual license because of the sacrifice of other communities. The spirit functions against historical blindness by opening the eyes of interpreters about their true locations within the social and economic worlds. Why is it necessary to posit spirit for this movement from semiotic blindness toward semiotic openness? (Corrington, 2000, p. 212; Shults, 2010)

The reason has to do with the kind of inertia found in psychosemiotic structures, which will usually let their own sign systems open without external and troublesome interference from contrary sign systems. When an alien and painful sign system threatens to intrude on self-understanding, the self has inherent mechanisms for pushing it away, with resistance being the strongest. Only the spirit, while finite in traditional senses, is large enough to invite the self into the space where an encounter with contrary material can take place. In this respect, the spirit is what opens the self and its relevant community, to its own past in such a way that it participates in the ambiguities still existing in the present. The spirit is thus an agent of linking, making the possibility of creative historical retrieval available to the self in the process (Corrington, 1992b, 2000; Shults, 2010)

For our church community, the first step in launching an anti-racism campaign is to turn the search light inward to acknowledge the ways in which racism marks the very empowerment structures that the community has taken for granted, perhaps for centuries. The spirit is like an agency that walks into the interpretive spaces among the members of the community, enabling the community to expel its false self-image as already being anti-racist.

The spirit is deeply connected to the principle of ontological parity. Whereas there is no direct correlation between the strict philosophical usages of the concept of parity, there is an analogical use in the political and social orders. If the concept of self-organization needs that of pluralistic democracy, then the concept of parity indirectly requires a conception of justice as long as the concept of justice confirms that all selves are equally real. Here there is a moral implication in the doctrine of ontological parity. There can be no priority schemes in which one group of selves is less real than another. The spirit then is one of the agencies of the sense of ontological parity in the social and political orders of interaction. The spirit makes it possible for our religious community to accept its own built-in priority schemes, and to recognize that they have caused great pain to other members of the larger community. In even more concrete terms, an immature community of interpreters can expose itself to witnesses who can testify to the effects of racism. To comprehend that racism even exists, it is necessary to see its direct effects on those for whom its force has long held sway. This is one of the hows of spirit; namely to provide an energy for this encounter that can still the flight-response that comes from a hidden guilt (Corrington, 1988, 1990b, 1993a, 2000).

However, the experience of compassion can quickly become romanticized or even degenerate into a form of the will to power in so far as compassion might entail the greater strength of the person who is in the privileged position of having compassion. How does the spirit make it possible for our religious community to move toward the positive momentum of anti-racism once it has made it possible for the community and its members to understand its own implied racism? Here again, the unique betweenness structures occupied by the spirit come into action.

Psychosemiotic structures is similar to physical bodies in that they have a kind of inertia that is a tendency to travel in the same direction unless acted upon by another force. Unlike more physical structures, however, psychosemiotic ones also have a sense that some other semiotic forces are a threat to the reigning self-image. The movement of the spirit has already made it possible for our community to integrate the painful sign series pointing to its own racism. However, the spirit has a second way of walking into the immature community of interpreters as it struggles to become a truly emancipator community (Corrington, 1988, 1994).

Tillich made a very clear correlation between the concept of courage, which is based on his ontological foundation, and the religious life (Tillich, 1952). In the current context, his formulation can be transformed to show how the spirit has its own power to insert something like this ontological and moral courage into a community to take on emancipator energies, even if they are against its own short-term interests (Tillich,

1952; Corrington, 2000, p. 214).

The spirit is anti-entropic in a sense. It does not live depending on some other order's resources, thus making it unique in its ontological status. This makes spirit a product of nature or an order with given locations within nature natured. If the self usually overcomes its own entropic decay dependent on other selves or other extra-human orders, it needs something that is differently anti-entropic if it is to enter into moral space. However, this also applies differently to those selves who have traditionally been the ones whose energy has been taken by other communities and selves. The return of more stable anti-entropic energy is from the spirit, which can give power to the self in the down position toward a renewal of energies that cannot be taken, at least initially from selves in the up position. The spirit lives naturally in the betweenness structures that have their own gradients which can become available to sign users under any conditions (Corrington, 2000, pp. 214-215).

The spirit does not need to be conscious of these gradients any more than water needs to know where to flow across a complex terrain (Corrington, 2000, p. 215). Traditionally, naturalism has been hostile to any concept of the spirit, if it is not that of Santayana's more harmless quasi-psychological one. The question can be raised: whether the spirit is singular in the sense being proffered by ecstatic naturalism. Traditionally the Western monotheisms rejected the idea that the spirit could be plurally located or could actually be plural in itself. In Christianity, the spirit was raised up to the status of the movement of Christ in time, so that without the spirit, the kingdom of god could not be actualized in history. Earlier notions of the spirit were held to be too linked o primitive forms of animism, or to be ancestor-centered rather than centered in the one true deity who has absolute sovereignty over all that occur in the world. Therefore, the spirit has had to play a role to which it was not ultimately fit. While it had to be a person co-equal to the divine at least in Christianity, it had to be more directly relevant to worldly orders and forms of psychosemiosis that were deeply fragmented and resistant (Corrington, 1992b, 2000).

Could this awareness be related to another which knows that not all manifestations of the spirit move in the same direction or have the same moral force? A question about this insight can be posed like the following: "how do you test the spirit to see if it is genuine? Was a form of the spirit manifest to Beethoven when he struggled, in spite of his manic-depressive disorder, to honor his sense of the divine through musical contrivance?" (Corrington, 1992b, 2000, p. 216).

The term spirit can be used in innumerable situations, many of which are incompatible with each other. However, what are the ontological structures regarding the spirit? It should be manifest that there may be a way to talk about spirit in itself provided that the complexities of the human/spirit correlation are never ignored. The following questions can be raised: "what are the marks of genuine spirit, and do these marks point to an ontological unity or an ontological plurality for the spirit?" The current perspective asserts that the spirit deals with the human process in a way that nature cannot as the sheer availability and unavailability of orders. This concern is primarily proven in its gift of ontological courage that enables the sign using self to look into its own unconscious projections and to acquire emancipator energies that may be available to its relevant communities. The grace of the spirit is thus different from natural grace which conveys bare-bones sense of prevalence. The unique grace of the spirit privileges the self as an individual toward its own selving process and the selving processes of others (Corrington, 1992b, 1993b, 2000, p. 217).

Where the spirit is located is morally ambiguous, because the spirit never acts alone but only within and against inertial structures that exert varying degrees of resistance. The spirit, which is naturally located and limited in such a way, simply cannot throw away all impediments to its unfolding. However, within an ambiguous situation, the universalizablity criterion can be applied so that moral energies can be mobilized to reduce the ambiguity and give the situation more moral.

The more difficult question is associated with the real or alleged unity of the spirit. Do we have to accept the reigning historical narrative which regards the principle of unity as an emergent from the inferior and dangerous principle of plurality? Should these two concepts always be used in their traditional ways? The ordinal perspective provides us another way of talking about the spirit that may reduce this tension. Considering the finite locatedness of the spirit, and the fact that its manifestation is always ambiguous in at least some aspects there might be no conceptual warrant or phenomenological evidence for continuing to talk about the spirit (Corrington, 2000, p. 218).

If various arguments and descriptions of the correlation of the human unconscious and the underconscious of nature are reasonable, it should follow that the spirit must come from the deepest recesses of the unconscious, and the spirit must come from somewhere below what we almost always mean by the human. If we accept its extra-human status and forms of locatedness, we can certainly make the easier assumption that the spirit is at least plural in its manifestations as these manifestations are assimilated by the self. If the manifestations of the spirit are always ambiguous, can we go even further and argue that some of them may entail that the spirit is at war with itself? This move was made in a different Trinitarian context with itself by Jung, who asserted that the biblical god manifest an internal psychological split between his own shadow projection of power onto Job and an internal image of righteousness. Jung argued that Job's steadfastness eventually, that is, by the New Testament, forced god to recognize this split within him and to overcome it by taking back the shadow projection on the cross. Jung's model has profound implications and represents one of those moments when psychoanalysis can open up the beginnings of a post monotheistic and universalistic perspective on the sacred (Corrington, 2000; Kerr, 1993).

It would be better to say here that the spirit is a postconsciousness rather than a split consciousness. In other words, a form of awareness is not split into halves so much as it is an awareness that at least has its own way of recognizing the limitations of conscious selves. In Tillichian language, it cannot be less than personal, but it is not a person. Therefore, it doesn't retain person-like features but it must be more than personal, and then simply adds new ones to its contour. It is a response that involves an unfolding of meaning, of furthering the growth of sign roots and blooms, of sign series, and of maximizing the scope density equation in pertinent orders of relevance, under the conditions of finitude.

In the world we live in is it meaningful to have a utopian longing in which each self would fulfill its selving process? How can we assume that there would be a convergence among these processes, such that even my genuine sense of selving would not conflict with someone else's? The hope that drives ecstatic naturalism is that the kind of postconsciousness that may be part of the elusive what of the spirit is somehow open to the need to reduce the clashes among selves when they involve the deeper unconscious components of the selving process. How can we assume that there would be a convergence among these processes, such that even my genuine sense of selving would not conflict with someone postconsciousness that may be part of the elusive what of the spirit is somehow open to the need to reduce the clashes among selves when they involve the deeper unconscious components of the selving process. But there we are pulled to the absolute edges of thought and experience, a realm where moral persuasion and rhetoric has usually replaced conceptual insight (Corrington, 1988, 1992b, 2000).

In this regard, the tentative assertions may be made. That is, the spirit is a kind of postconsciousness: "1) that is plurally located at least 2) that always appears in ambiguous ways in ambiguous situations 3) that has its own moment pointing toward some form of universality and parity, 4) human process which may cut across cost-benefit analyses 5) that lives in between's structures 6) that aids the interpretive processes of interpretive and emancipator communities, and 7) that provides the gift of ontological courage to human sign users. Given all of these traits of the spirit, are we now ready to make a statement concerning it real or alleged unity?" (Corrington, 2000, pp. 221-222)

If ambiguity is not a trait that only emerges for human sign users, but an ontological structure, can the spirit occupy an unambiguous perch to overcome ambiguity? The spirit should in itself be ambiguous in its ontological structure, although it is much less ambiguous than we are. This ambiguity presupposes that there is some ontological conflict within the spirit that is not fully consistent with itself.

It seems to be clear that the spirit should traverse a complex terrain that it itself did not make, because the concept of creation is here considered purely intra-worldly and finite. Insofar as any momentum across a terrain denotes some minimal sense of awareness of that terrain at least for the spirit, which is post conscious, then it follows that there will be terrain-dependent traits that are part of the spirit. As discussed earlier, the spirit is anti-entropic on its own, but it should also live in entropic orders and assimilate their entropy in a certain respect. Therefore, the spirit accepts entropy into its evolving contour, even if it will be subject to entropy in a different way, for it has principles of organization that are preordinal and presemiotic (Corrington, 1992b, 1993b, 2000).

The spirits that are so clearly manifest in sacred folds within nature are infinite. They have no collective contour that could be mapped, and there is no divine being of all beings who could even map them. They are truly emergent from the underconscious of nature and are themselves unaware of what lies in this underconscious.

Hartshorne has suggested a god that is infinitely self-surpassable, but he has not provided a clear explanation of what makes that surpassability possible. What provides the space for its own growth is nature rather than the divine itself both in its inexhaustible underconscious dimension and in its unlimited orders of so-called creation. The concept of the divine itself is still so full of anthropomorphic structures necessary to give way to a concept of the sacred. In this sense, Hartshorne has not made a claim about anything like self-consciousness and intentionality. However, in forming his neo-classical theism, Hartshorne (1948) has enabled a more daring philosophical theology to explore a different way of understanding the growth and decay of the sacred, a unique way of understanding the growth and decay of the sacred, a his own way of understanding an incomplete divinity that is in need of orders other than itself (Corrington, 1992b, 1993b, 2000).

The sacred is self-surpassble but it seems to be vulnerable to entropic decay. It was claimed that the archetypes as pre-semiotic and semiotic both were greater in scope and power than the sacred orders or traits that appeared within their provenance. This setting for the sacred, that is, this basis of the underconscious of nature and its potencies, pulls philosophical theology, as a reflection on and a response to sacred orders of relevance. Clearly the sacred orders that we encounter are composed of human projections, but they are also more than some of those projections and less than others. Ultimately, in accordance with ecstatic naturalism, the sacred orders are more than projections and less than fully divine in the monotheistic sense. The spirits that combine into a variety of forms from human artifacts to numinous locations within physical nature take the human process in powerful ways, leading the processes of semiosis into more capacious horizons of meaning that are at least potentially universal and filled with a sense of parity. However, it is not at all clear that all of these spirit-enhanced locations can be impossible. The sign systems of one location, which are filled with spiritual energy, may be hostile to the sign systems of another. In fact, the spirits that enter into the world of psychosemiosis are often both conflictual and ambiguous in their manifestations. (Corrington, 2000, pp. 224-225).

The spirits emerging from their own betweenness structures enter into semiotic relations with attained sign systems. Spirits have a momentum that pushes any semiotic system toward the edges of its own stability order so that a creative disorder may emerge. Along with this change to the plural language of spirits, the two criteria of universalizability and the sense of parity are fully applicable. The current perspective says that the thing is always far more than it appears and that the implications of psychoanalysis force us to investigate what those hidden facets and implications are. The thing is actually as static as it seems and has its own restlessness, on the basis of the presemiotic. Every categorical structure carries the shadows of its own rejection and the most important phenomenological work is often done in this realm (Corrington, 1992b, 1993b, 2000).

The spirits of nature are thus infused into sacred folds and manifest themselves to those with the sensitivity to understand their unique ontological location as emergent from the structures of betweenness. Particular concrescences come and go subject to their own form of entropy but the spiritual powers behind them are not as directly entropic. For our own species, the entropic quality of the spirits is almost negligible. However, we must live with the fact that all manifestations are entropic regardless of our cultic practices. What is clear is that within the brief trajectory of any life, a sacred fold may be quite stable and enduring in its ability to sustain semiotic energies against the entropy coming from the non-spiritual orders of the world (Corrington, 1992b, 1993a, 2000).

Thus far we have looked at religion and signs, especially focusing on Perice's triadic semiotics, Neville's religious symbolism, and Corrington's semiosis of world and the meaning evolution before discussing semiosis of African American religion in chapter IV and V. Religion is an on-going semiotic process where interpreters select paradigmatic elements to form syntagmatic combinations. This religious semiosis tends to take the form of conflicts. Following Peirce's triadic semiotics, in the African American religion, Firstness is associated with the harsh reality which African Americans have confronted since slavery, and the feeling which they have had in undergoing and overcoming their adversity. Secondness in the semiotics of African American religion is related to their reaction to ruthless reality and their way to surmount their distress. Thirdness in the triadic relation of African American religion is related to their recognition, thoughts and self-consciousness of their reality or difficulties. Based on this Peirce's triadic semiotics and religious symbolism, i.e. the assumption that religious symbols have an interpretative, practical and transformative function, we will investigate the dynamic phenomena of African American religion, that is, semiosis of African American religion in the following chapters.

03

Historical overview of African American Religion

African American religion is not a unified phenomenon but a very diverse reality in organizational, historical, sociological, theological, and liturgical forms. This vast diversity reflects the influence of massive demographic shifts in the African American population from the rural south to southern, western and northern cities between the first and second World Wars. Since the late eighteenth century onward, however, the vast majority of African Americans have adhered to their own modified forms of independent Protestantism. Its rapid growth evidenced their collective response to the racist thought and practices of the Euro-American churches. Therefore, one cannot overestimate the historical importance of African-American religion in their public life. During two and a half centuries of slavery followed by another century of racial discrimination and segregation, African slaves in America struggled tirelessly for the eventual realization of freedom. They were denied the right of full citizenship by the constitution of the nascent republic and despite the 13th, 14th, and 15th constitutional amendments, the right was denied twice by the U.S. Supreme Court: first in the 1846 Dred Scott decision and second, in the 1896 Plessy v Ferguson decision. The long journey of African Americans to citizenship was finally accomplished with the passage of the Civil Rights Act of 1964 and the Voting Rights Act of 1965. It is irony that a people who was formerly known as Africans in America and degraded by such racial designations as Colored or Negro now accepts their self-proclaimed hybrid name, African American. (See Johnson, 2007; Paris, 2008, p. 475)

African slaves could only assemble clandestinely during slavery, but they succeeded even under the conditions of bondage to organize their own public realm, the "invisible church", what E. Franklin Frazier called in that it had been invisible only to whites. In the sacred places, black slaves expressed their humanity by establishing a surrogate world. Their clandestine world was firmly rooted in a religio-social vision of how humans should live together. In those places they worshipped their God by integrating African and Christian understandings and practices, and they developed the lyrics and music for what were later called the spirituals. This church provided the African slaves with mutual support systems that helped them undergo horrible reality during slavery (Raboteau, 1980, 1994).

The consistent exercise of the practices in the African American church gradually resulted in the development of a slave community, which displayed a strong sense of social and communal cohesion recalling their respective tribal communities in Africa. Undergoing the racial oppression and the gradual loss of their specific tribal and familial identities in the African homeland, their religious communities soon became primary sources of personal strength and encouragement as well as communal sources for socioeconomic development, self-respect, and racial pride (Raboteau, 1980, 1994; Johnson, 2007; Paris, 2008).

In the late eighteenth century, freed slaves founded the first independent black church in the city of Philadelphia. Indeed, the 1792 exodus of Richard Allen and others from St. George's Methodist Church in Philadelphia marked the crucial turning point in the history of African American religious and cultural development. It expressed the beginning of a major religious movement among freed African Americans that eventually resulted in the formation of the various African American denominations. Even though a number of African churches existed prior to that time in the slave-holding states, they were invariably subject to the supervision of their white overseers. Thus, under the conditions of freedom first in northern cities, the natural human desire to form communities expressed itself as an act of protest against the discriminatory and segregationist practices of white racism (Paris, 2008, P. 476). Rather, Africans universally criticized the use of race as a principle of exclusion and subordination. In fact, their effort to be independent from their Euro-American parent churches constituted a necessary means by which they could manifest their rejection to comply with the racist practices of the Euro-American churches (Johnson, 2007; Paris, 2008).

African Americans were forced theologically and morally not to accept and conform what they thought of as the racist practices of the racists. By doing so, they institutionalized a non-racist principle based on their doctrine of God as impartial parent of all peoples which signified the kinship of all peoples. The public act of distancing themselves from the communal practice of racism enabled the African American churches take the public transformational role at the moment of their birth. The originating principle made it possible to offer an independent space for their people to worship God and serve all the needs of their people according to their own desires and choices. The practice of improving both the spiritual and material well-being of African peoples, whether free or enslaved, represented their uniqueness. African American church solely gave primacy to the well-being of African Americans. Thus, these African American churches played a leading role in performing multidimensional roles and functions in serving all the needs of their peoples (Raboteau, 1980, 1994; Johnson, 2007; Paris, 2008).

African American churches founded schools, colleges, seminaries, hospitals, publishing houses, newspapers, insurance companies, banks, burial societies, businesses, social clubs, and civil rights organizations, etc. Moreover, these churches established the basic moral values of the African American community, formed the ethos for social order and cohesion, and offered the role models for community leadership. In fact, for generations these churches provided the primary training ground for ecclesiastical, political, economic, social, and educational leadership. The talents of professional singers, musicians, artists, teachers, social workers, business entrepreneurs, and civil rights leaders were first recognized by their churches which provided them the necessary support and encouragement (See Gadzekpo, 2001; Lincoln & Mamiya, 1990; Paris, 2008).

In the nineteenth and twentieth centuries also, the African American churches played an essential role in leading both the individual and collective lives of their people in a decent way. Their commitment to the good of the African American community has been the principal reason why the African American churches have flourished so well from one generation to another. The black churches only provided their peoples with opportunities for leadership, moral development, self-respect, and racial pride. They alone gave courage in the midst of hostile environments. However, their mission was variously understood by their many leaders. In fact, the diverse courageous deeds virtually made them legends in their own time (See Johnson, 2007; Paris, 2008).

Moreover, during the past two centuries, African American religious institutions have played leading roles in establishing the foundation for the social organization of the African American community and in pursuing racial justice. Their social actions have taken a variety of forms that have ranged along the following political continuum from the right to the left wings of the political spectrum: i) racial self-development plans aimed at maintaining and enhancing their humanity under the conditions of racial injustice; ii) a socially adaptive plan that correlates well with that of Booker T. Washington's post-reconstruction activities at Tuskegee, that is, the plan promoting hard work, moral development, entrepreneurial success, and the privatization of both religion and politics; iii) political reform in government that is associated with that of Reconstruction of religio-political leadership of Henry McNeil Turner and the mid-twentieth century leadership of Adam Clayton Powell, Jr.; iv) an action which seeks to use electoral politics as a tool for racial justice; v) legitimate public protest activities which are related to that of W.E.B. DuBois's work in founding and providing leadership for the National Association for the Advancement of Colored People and, similarly, with the work of Martin Luther King, Jr. and the Southern Christian Leadership Conference that give primacy to the quest for racial and social justice while seeking to build a society in accordance with the dictates of peace among all peoples; vi) radical nationalist activities that view the nation as incurably racist and bent on preserving all systems of racial injustice which correlated with that of the back to Africa movements under the leadership of such persons as Malcolm X, Louis Farrakan, and the Nation of Islam; vii) a style of Albert Cleague and The Church of the Black Madonna that has inspired considerable creativity in literature, music, art, and religion as evidenced in this post-civil rights era with the rise of black power, black theology, womanist thought, and Afro-centricity (See Swain, 2008, Paris, 2008, pp. 478- 479).

African Americans had their first experience of citizenship during the brief period known as the Reconstruction (1865-1877). After its collapse in 1877 they lost all such rights and they have not had the rights throughout the first half of the twentieth century. From then on, African American churches tried to improve their rights within their racially proscribed world by moral suasion but did not succeed in changing the system of racial discrimination and segregation. (Paris, 2008, p. 479)

Based on the legacy of the past, African American churches challenged and inspired the hearts and minds of millions of people for a decade. Its philosophy of non-violent direct resistance expressed the courageous and reconciling spirit, which was embodied by the black churches. The consistency of its practice in the midst of terror and death gradually helped the nation understand and solve the problem it had created. In brief, the so-called civil rights movement represented the rebirth of African American religion in the public domain. In fact, C. Eric Lincoln asserted that that period represented a watershed moment that actually changed the so-called "Negro Church" into the "Black Church" because it was the first time that the church had militantly confronted the established powers of racial injustice and succeeded in winning the victory (See Gadzekpo, 2001; Lincoln & Mamiya, 1990).

The 1964 Civil Rights Act and the Voter's Rights Act of 1965 ended the church's long, arduous struggle for civil rights. Insofar as the struggle formed the primary public mission of the African American churches, its civil rights victory had a significant effect on the on-going internal life of the churches themselves. Clearly the achievement implied a necessary change in the form and content of their public ministries. They could not rely on the universal African American consensus against legally proscribed racism in the nation's civil life as their primary focus. In some important ways the civil rights movement in the United States was similar to the independence movements in Africa. Consequently, the post-civil rights period in America may be considered analogous to the post-independence period in Africa. First, although lingering forms of the former eras remain in both situations, the older forms of social analysis are no longer appropriate even if all new forms of racial injustice show both continuities and discontinuities with the older forms (See Swain, 2008; Paris, 2008).

Second, as many post-independence leaders in Africa have tended to become corrupt, a similar destiny can befall post-civil rights leaders in the United States as well. In the post-civil rights era, the primary public mission of African American churches may be classified in the following ways: (a) providing various kinds of membership services e.g., doing what they had always done in trying to meet the needs of their members by distributing food and clothing; comforting the sick, the elderly, and the dying; promoting mutual support programs); programs for all ages such as gospel singing, liturgical dance, religious drama; recreational events; local, regional, and national assemblies. (b) organizing various types of community service programs: i.e., credit unions, unemployment services, catering meals, day-care centers, church sponsored day schools, after-school programs, Saturday schools, health fairs; senior citizens' homes; allowing their properties to be used by community organizations such as Alcohol Anonymous Twelve-Step Program; Ten-step Programs, organizations for the blind and the deaf; etc. (c) integrating African American religion with Afrocentric cultural esthetics to help African Americans develop a stronger sense of pride in their

African identity by adapting selected African traditions for liturgical, cultural and psychological purposes: e.g., Kwanza celebration, wearing African apparel, adopting African names, African liturgical dance, rites of passage programs especially for youth, group visits to Africa, etc. (d) building political and para-political organizations: i.e., providing resources of space, programs, and volunteers for political campaigning, on-going support of traditional civil rights organizations, black colleges, black businesses, The Children's Defense Fund, and ad hoc responses to racially inspired civic outrages; (e) developing ecumenical and other types of coalitions: i.e., inter-denominational ministers' alliances/fellowships, national and world councils of churches, forming independent not-for-profit subsidiaries for governmental funding purposes; and other community service projects. (Paris, 2008, p. 481)

Thus, one can easily see the wide range of social, political, and communal practices in which the African American churches have continued to be involved. However, the extent and intensity of their involvement remains unclear and therefore, needs more scholarly analysis and precise measurement. The symbolic power of African American religion can help inspire Church members to become more aware of their Christian responsibility to the poor and those in need of advocacy. In addition to it, the social and communal programs of the African American churches have more effect on the basic problems facing the African American community as a whole. In the twenty first century, a basic question that the African American churches confronts is whether the African American churches thrive in the twenty first century as well as they have in the latter half of the twentieth century? The importance of this question should not be underestimated (See Paris, 2008; Lincoln &Mamiya, 1990).

04

African American Religion during slavery

1. Backgrounds of Christianizing Slaves

Jon Butler (1990) argued that there was a "Spiritual holocaust" in colonial America, that is, the obliteration of African culture and religion when the slaves arrived at America. Butler saw secular apprehension in obliteration African religion in America: "Throughout the colonial period planters worried about collective slave activity of any kind. "Slave control was based on the eradication of all forms of African culture because whites had fear of cultural power to unify the slaves and enable them to resist or rebel.[1]

1 http : // www.mediapro.net/cdadesign/paine/afri.html

White Americans thought of African religion as "false" religion believing in devil. The evil rituals threatened the people trying to stamp them out. The first and instinctive response to foreign religion was not merely "prejudice" but also a wish to convert. It was self-defense. African religion was repressed so reflexively that there is little evidence of the process. It was too clear to those who enacted it for them to articulate a rationale for discussion. It literally "went without saying" that diabolic religions must be crushed and converted (See Cade, 1935; Butler, 1990).

Once the slaves' religion was expelled, their conversion to Christianity caused the problem of treating one's property as one's brother or sister in Christ. It was a great problem even in Christianity's earliest days when white Christians found it unnecessary to plan long social reforms like the ending of slavery. However, pangs of guilt over enslaving fellow Christians were lessened by stressing the grace of faith made available to Africans, who otherwise would die as pagans.

Most American slave owners did not want to make their slaves part of themselves by baptism. In fact, they would prefer to think of their slaves as alien. However, it was impossible to allow an alien religion to exist in a people within the owners' domain. Besides, if false religion was quashed among the Africans, it was hard to oppose those Christian preachers saying that the true religion must replace it. If a spiritual vacuum had been created, it must be filled (Fowler, 1985).

According to Herskovits (1970), white slave holders thought that: (1) blacks are childlike by nature; and the genetically inferior to whites; (2) there was no uniting ethos for the enslaved blacks who came from all quarters of Africa; (3) the slaves are people without a past because slavery thoroughly emaciated that past assigning it to nonexistence. Given all of this, Whites also thought that Christianity could be used as an instrument of control as long as passages on slave obedience were taught as central to it. They attempted to teach slaves the epistles of Paul: "slaves, be obedient to your masters." (Fowler, 1985, p. 197) This went against true Christians using the gospel as apolitical charter of freedom and the belief that the Christian religion could be made to mean different things. Despite this variety in the forms of faith, could slave holders be sure that the religion they preached would continue to be the religion slaves would observe?

2. Difficulties in Slave Conversion During the First Century of Slavery

2.1 Slave Holders

Despite the widely held justification of slavery as a means of preaching the gospel and declarations of the duty of Christian colonists to Christianize the pagans, the process of slave conversion was blocked by many obstacles in the first century of slavery: slave holders' objection, slave's unwillingness to conversion and unsettled religious situation.

English colonists did not want to Christianize their slaves due to the fear that baptism would emancipate their slaves. Slave holders widely believed that if slaves were baptized, "they should according to the laws of the British nation, and the canons of its church, be freed, even if the notion was legally vague" (Raboteau, 1980, p. 98).The Christian mission to spread the gospel to all nations confronted the economic interest of the Christian slave holders. Their top priority was not the Christianization of their slaves but the economic profitability of the slaves.

This dilemma was solved by colonial legislation obliging Negroes to serve duration of life. In 1664 the lower house of Maryland asked the upper house "to draw up an Act obliging negroes to serve durante vita··· for the prevention of the damage Maters of such Slaves must susteyne by such Slaves pretending to be christened[;] and so pleade the lawe of England." By 1706 at least six colonial legislatures had passed acts denying that baptism changed the condition of a slave "as to his bondage of freedom". Even after colonial assemblies had declared that baptism was no threat to a planter's legal right to hold Negroes in perpetual bondage, the process of religious instruction which had to precede baptism was seen by many slave holders as an economic detriment (Fauset, 1971; Morgan et. al., 1997, p. 110).

It took time for a slave to be catechized adequately whereas plantation work schedule gave the slave little time for religious instruction. Sunday was the only possible day for instruction but slaves had to work on Sunday either for their masters of for themselves. Influenced by missionaries in America and by officials in London, some governors urged colonial legislatures to pass bills stopping masters from working slaves on Sunday or otherwise blocking their attendance (Klingberg, 1941, p. 7). Even though legislation might have revised a slave holders' behavior, it did not change his attitude against the instruction of slaves.

Slave holders were divided in their views about slave religion. Some slave holders promoted Christianity among their slaves. The ways in which slaves could be formally acquainted with Christianity among their slaves can be found in the comments of ex-slaves from Alabama. Molly Ammonds said that her master built his slaves a church with a floor and seats and the top was covered with pine boughs in which the master's father would preach. Other masters cared little as to whether their slaves had religion. These masters were less concerned about the amusements and religion of their slaves as long as they did not affect his working ability.

Some masters thought that Africans were incapable of instructions, and therefore, they objected to slave conversion. Their notion was based on the linguistic and cultural barriers between African-born slaves and English colonists. Some planters even went further than that. They objected to slave conversion not only because of cultural differences but also because of racial distinctions. The famous philosopher Bishop Berkeley complained in 1731 about the American colonists that their "ancient antipathy to the Indians···together with an irrational contempt for the Blacks, as creatures of another species, who had no right to be instructed or admitted to the sacraments; has proved a main obstacle to the conversion of these poor people." (Raboteau, 1980, pp. 100-102; Raboteau, 2000)

The most serious obstacle to the missionary's access to the slaves was the master's vague notion that a Christian slave would have some claim to fellowship, which would threaten the security of the master-slave hierarchy. Even after other fears could be alleviated by legislation or by arguments, unease with the concept of spiritual equality between master and slave caused slave holders to object to slave conversion. Peter Kalm, a Swedish traveler in American from 1748-50, described the masters' fears that Christianity would destroy their relationship their slaves;

> It is likewise greatly to be pitied, that the masters of these Negroes in the most of the English colonies take little cave of their spiritual welfare, and let them live on in Pagan darkness. There are even some, who would be very ill pleased at, and would by all means hinder their negroes from being instructed in the doctrines of Christianity; to this they are partly led by the

> conceit of its being shameful to have a spiritual brother or sister among so despicable a people; partly by thinking that they should not be able to keep their Negroes, so meanly afterwards; and partly through fear of the Negroes growing too proud, on seeing themselves upon a level with their masters in religious matters is (Kalm, 1773, p. 503)

In addition, masters complained that Christianity would ruin their slaves by making them "saucy" since they would begin to think themselves equal to whites (Morgan et al., 1997, p. 410). Slave holders had fear that Christianity would make their slaves proud, ungovernable and even rebellious.

2.2 Religious Situation

The opposition of slave holders was not the only factor obstructing the conversion of slaves. Part of the problem was the religious situation itself. In the Southern colonies where slaves were largely concentrated, the religious situation was unsettled. Clergy were insufficient. Even in Virginia, where the established church of England "was on its firmest footing, in 1701 nearly half of the forty to forty-six parishes containing 40,000 people were not supplied with Clergy." In 1724 Hugh Jones reported that North Carolina needed missionaries "not only for the Conversion of the Indians and Baptism of Negroes there, but for the Christening and Recovery to the Practical Profession of the Gospel great numbers of English that have but the bare name of God and Christ." (Raboteau, 180, pp. 104-105; Raboteau, 2000)

When ministers were present, they found themselves taking care of parish of vast size. Because of long distances to travel, danger from illness and disease, and the unsettled character of colonial life, the Anglican clergy often depended on or were controlled by the local vestry and the planter class, for the their living and status. In addition, since the closest bishop was in London, the established church was in no position to execute its policy with regard to slave conversion in the colonial South (Raboteau, 1980, pp. 105-106; Raboteau, 2000).

Moreover, it was most problematic the way in which the process of Christianization was carried out by the missionaries. The Church of England emphasized religious instruction in its efforts to convert the slaves. An example of this catechetical method was described by Francis Le Jan in 1710:

> Since it has pleased Almighty God to bless me with health I have upon Sundays after out divine service, invited the negores and Indian slaves to stay for half an hour··· We begin and end out particular assembly with the Collect Prevent us O Lord etc. I teach them the Creed, the Lord's Prayer and the Commandments. I explain some portion of the catechism. I give them an entire liberty to ask questions. I endeavor to proportion my answers and all my instructions to their want and capacity (Raboteau, 1980, p. 116).

The Anglican catechist believed that eventually religious instruction should include teaching the slaves to read. One of the first Society for the Propagation of the Gospel (SPG) missionaries sent to the colonies, Samuel Thomas of Goose Creek, South Carolina, automatically accepted a connection between Christian initiation and slave literacy when he reported in 1702 that he had taught twenty slave to read while instruction them in the Christian faith. The tendency to regard the religious instruction of slaves as equal to education led to sponsor several Negro schools in the colonies. However, usual problems such as vehement objections from some planters, inability to communicate with African slaves, and irregular attendance resulted in the failure of public school. The notion of colonial protestants, whether Anglican, Puritan, Baptist, or Quaker as well as the Church of England, that conversion is a process of religious instruction did not boost slave conversion, rather discouraged it (Klingberg, 1941, pp. 105-108; Mays & Nicholson, 1933).

2.3 Slaves

The slaves' response to conversion into Christianity was various but it was always conditioned by the circumstances of slavery. There was something strange about the way African slaves were Christianized in America. Traditionally "preaching the gospel to all nations" meant that a Christian disciple was sent out with the gospel to the pagans (Raboteau, 1980, p. 120). In America the reverse happened: the pagan slave was brought to a Christian disciple who was frequently reluctant to instruct him in the gospel. The irony of that situation had practical implications for the interrelationships among master, missionary, and slave.

While conversion was regarded as a process of religious instruction there were linguistic and cultural barriers between African-born slaves and European masters. It is clear from the reports of S.P.G. that they had little success with African-born slaves. Sharp distinctions were also made between imported Negroes and 'native-born' slaves. The bishop did not understand that the degree of fluency in English necessary for an African slave to "get by" in the "ordinary business" of plantation life was not high enough to understand an explanation of Christian doctrine. In addition, not all slaves who could understand religious instruction were eager to accept Christianity. William Tibbs, of St. Paul's Parish Baltimore Country Maryland reported in 1724 that he had baptized and taught some slaves but most slaves refused instruction (Raboteau 1980, p. 120; Raboteau, 2000).

The most significant reason for the slaves to refuse religious instruction and conversion was that baptism did not lead to their instruction and did not allow slaves themselves to have freedom. As the legislation served economic benefits of slaveholder, slaves lost their hopes and were not motivated to conversion. Also the slaves themselves could not but be sensitive to the hypocrisy of masters. Rev Francis Varnod minister to St. Geothe's Parish in south Carolina said in 1724 that the slaves "were also sensible that as we are Christians, we do not act accordingly upon which account a negro by about 14 who has never been instructed, being blamed by his mistress (as she was aging to church), for some things he had done amiss. Was heard to say, my mistress can curse and go to Church…" (Klingberg, 1941, p. 56; Raboteau, 2000).

Even though the slaves received religious instructions their response to instruction and reading was not always what the missionaries had hoped. Rev, Le Jau described in al letter a disturbing incident.

> The best scholar of all the Negroes in my parish and a very sober and honest liver through his learning was like to create some confusion among all the Negroes in this country. Ha had a book wherein he read some description of the several judgments that chastise men because of their sins in these latter days that description made an impression upon his spirit and he told his master abruptly there would be a dismal time and the moon would be turned into blood and there would be dearth of darkness and went away… but when he spoke these few words to his manner some negro overheard a part and it was publicly blazed abroad that an angel came and spoke to the man. He had seen a hand that gave him a book; he had heard voices, seen fires, etc. As I had opportunities I took care to undeceive those who asked me about it… (Klingberg, 1941, pp. 46-47)

Catechesis moved in two directions. The slaves were taught the prayers, doctrines and rites of Christian belief and ritual if instruction was to become more than mere parroting. Since the slaves brought their cultural past to the task of translating and interpretation the doctrinal words and ritual gestures of Christianity, the meaning which the slaves actually found were different.

Thus, during the first century and a half of slavery in the U.S. only a small minority of slaves received instruction in the Christian faith. The objections of slaveholder; the unsettled religious situations in the Southern colonies in which a great majority of the slaves lived; the lack of missionaries to catechize slaves; linguistic and cultural barriers between Africans and Europeans; the very way in which conversion was generally perceived as catechesis, a long process of religious instruction; slave's unwillingness to conversion-all these factors ensured that progress in slave conversion was slow.

3. Revival and Conversion

3.1 Revival and Conversion

The Great Awakening represented "the dawning of the new day" in the history of slave conversion. Revival that initially swept over most of the British North America colonies in the

1740s spread to particularly Chesapeake region of the upper South during the 1780s and 1790s and to the Kentucky and Tennessee frontier around the turn of the century. Theses successive "Awakenings" initiated a new religious movement in America whether viewed as a renewed Puritanism, an extension of Continental Pietism or as the rise of popular denominations of the expanding frontier. Evangelicalism was by the early decades of the nineteenth century, the predominant voice on the American religious scene.[2]

Jonathan Edward said that revival of 1734-36 was affecting black churchgoers as well as whites: "There are several negroes who from what was seen in them and what is discernible in them since appear to have been truly born again in the late remarkable season."When the full tide of the Great Awakening swept over the colonies beginning in 1740 blacks were filled with religious excitement. Many African Americans adopted evangelical Christianity during the revivals of eighteenth and nineteenth centuries (Lutz, 2001). Whitefield, Tennent and other revivalists saw with satisfaction hundreds of black people flocking to hear their powerful message of Salvation. An Anglican clergyman in Salm, in Massachusetts reacted with disdain to the effect of the revival: "So great has been the enthusiasm created by Wesley and Whitefield and Tennent that people talk of nothing but *'renovation regeneration conviction and conversion'*…"[3]

---

2 http : //www.nhc.rtp.nc.us

Later in the eighteenth century African Americans whether slave or free, southern or northern, started to convert to Christianity in large numbers than ever before. The type of Christianity which they joined and continued to join in huge numbers was "experiential, regionalistic and biblically oriented". It stressed the necessity of an inward conversion experience for Christian salvation rather than religious instruction... Also it institutionalized the revival as a means of converting sinners, increasing church membership and reforming society (Raboteau, 1987, p. 92; Raboteau, 2000).

In the Southern colonies the revival impulse continued to "smolder and to flare up" sporadically under the preaching of evangelical ministers. Pro-revival, or New Light Presbyterians as well as Pro-revival or Separated Baptists and Methodists continued the work of the evangelicalism moving west with the frontier into the Old Southwest. (Boles, 1972, p. 10)

Presbyterian Samuel Davies, a leading New Light and future president of the College of New Jersey began his ministry to seven congregations in Hanover County, Virginia in 1748. Davies who respected education as characteristic of Presbyterians stressed the necessity to teach the slaves to read and had hoped to write "a book with the combined purpose of teaching reading and Christianity" but plan was never completed. The evangelical heart of Davies' message to the slaves was not religious instruction but the experience of con-

---

3 http : //www.nhc.rtp.nc.us

version as can be seen from his advice to black converts

> You will say perhaps "other negroes are baptized and why not I" but consider some other negroes have been I great trouble about their souls; their hearts have been broken for sin; they have accepted Christ as their only Savior and are Christians indeed; and when you are such it will be time enough for you to be baptized. (Pilcher, 1966, p. 300)

In 1786 the first year in which Methodists distinguished white and black members in their records, there were 1890 black members out of a total membership of 18,791 In 1797 the black membership stood at one-fourth of the total Methodist membership. One estimate is that in 1793 the black Baptist membership was about one-fourth the total membership of 73,471 or between 18000and 19000. Whereas these figures are probably inflated there is no doubt that the growth in black as well as white membership among the Baptists and Methodists was surprising (Sweet, 1952, pp. 277-278; Emerson & Smith, 2000). This surprising growth resulted from the religious fervor of revival.

The revivalist impulse of the Great Awakening spread to the frontier in 1800. The Great Western Revival, initiated by the Gaspar River and Cane Ridge camp meetings in Kentucky, embraced blacks who eagerly participated in the tumultuous exercise, characteristic of frontier revivalism (Sweet, 1952, p. 279). Thus theses successive revival was powerful in accelerating the pace of slave conversion.

3.2 Main Factors of the Increase in Conversion

The increase in conversion of Negroes under the impact of revivalism was due to several factors. The evangelical religion spread by the revivalist began a religious renaissance in the South where religious situation was unsettled. The revival itself became a means of church extension for Presbyterians, Methodists and Baptists. The mobility of the Methodists circuit rider and the local autonomy of the Baptist preacher were fitted to the needs and conditions of the rural South. In the heat of religious fervor, slave holders could not be indifferent about their own religious involvement and about that of their slaves as well (Raboteau, 1980, p. 297; Emerson & Smith, 2000).

The religious revivals were based on a practical Armianism: God would save all who believed in Him; salvation was there for all to hold if they would (Levine, 1977, p. 75; Emerson & Smith, 2000). Blacks thought of the experience of God's power as the norm of Christian truth rather than the Bible. For them the Bible followed conversion. 'They wanted to see their children and friends get religion as they did. They fell under the mighty power of God… after mourning many days, and then came out shouting, for an angel they said, told them their sins were forgiven. They said their masters and families were Bible Christians, and they did not want to be like them (Raboteau, 1987, pp. 97-98; Levine, 1977).

The individualistic emphasis of revivalism with its strong emphasis on inward conversion brought about egalitarianism. Many clergy promoted the idea that all Christians were equal in the sight of God, which provided hope and sustenance to the slaves. By heavily emphasizing the inward conversion experience, the Awakening tended to deemphasize the outward status of men which caused black and white alike to feel personally that Christ had died for them as individuals. Evangelical religion had a universal dimension which encouraged preaching to all men and embracing rich and poor, free and slave.

Evangelicals were as concerned as Anglicans about observing the rules of Christian conduct after conversion, but it was the experience of "conviction, repentance regeneration" that took the attention of the Evangelicals whereas the Anglican clergyman had a tendency to be "didactic and moralistic." The Methodist or Baptist exhorter visualized and personalized the drama of sin and salvation. That appeared a lot to black slaves. The revivalist preacher helped them feel the weight of sin, imagine the fears of Hell and accept Christ as their own Savior (Raboteau, 1980, pp. 132-133; Emerson & Smith, 2000; Harvey, 2005).

Emphasizing the conversion experience instead of the process of religious instruction allowed illiterate slaves more access to Christianity. The revivalists tried to minimize complicate explanations of doctrine. The intense concentration on conversion left little room for elaborate catechesis. The plain doctrine and heavy emotion of revivalist sermons appealed to the Black slave. The experience of John Tompson born as a slave in Maryland in 1812 is illustrated.

> …..But soon the Methodist religion was brought among us and preached in a manner so plain that the way farming man, though a fool could not err therein. This new doctrine produced great consternation among the slave holders. It was something which they could not understand. It brought glad tidings to the poor bondman; it bound up the broken-hearted, it opened the prison doors to them that were bound and let the captive go free. (Morton, 1941, pp. 239-242).

The Baptists and Methodists did not insist on a well-educated clergy. So they did not confront short supply in clergy. A converted heart and a gifted tongue were more important than how much theological training was received. If a converted slave showed talent for exhorting, he could exhort. The black exhorters and ministers were licensed to preach and they preached the gospel of spiritual freedom to the slaves. In 1798 a free Negro Joseph Willis who was a duty licensed Baptist preacher initiated his work in Southwest Mississippi. In 1804 he moved to Louisiana and in 1812 formed the state's first Baptist church at bayou Chicot, where he served as pastor. In Lexington Kentucky, a slave named "old captain" gathered a church in 1801 which eventually had over three hundred black members (Roboteau, 1980, pp. 133-134; Raboteau, 2000).

In slave conversion, it was more significant that black preachers, whether licensed or not, preached to slaves. They preached themselves to those of their own color, and in most cases their preaching was very useful even though it was broken and illiterate. Until several state legislatures passed laws forbidding Negroes to preach, the Baptist churches licensed and ordained black men who "felt the call" to preach after they showed their talents and proved their faith before a committee of the church. Slave preachers were allowed to preach only after they got permission from their owners and normally were restricted to the area of the local parish (Roboteau, 1980, pp. 135-138; Raboteau, 2000; Harvey, 2005). Nevertheless, blacks, in numbers not seen before, slave and free, attended revival meetings or Sabbath services and joined Methodist and Baptist Churches.

Even when the practice was illegal, the Methodists sent out black assistants with their itinerate preachers in a few cases. Methodists skirted legal restrictions against black preachers by simply licensing them as exhorters (Roboteau, 1980). The significance of theses early black preachers in the conversion of slaves to Christianity in the latter half of the eighteenth and the early decades of the nineteenth centuries could not overemphasized. They played an important role as crucial mediators between Christian beliefs and the experiential world of the slaves. In fact, they helped to develop a bicultural synthesis, an Afro-American culture by nurturing the birth of Christian communities among blacks.

05

Characteristics of African-American Religion

1. White Religion?

Blacks had heard the message of evangelical Christianity from whites in the beginning, but rapidly early black preachers, whether licensed or unlicensed, attempted to convert and to pastor their own people. By 1830 these "Pioneers" had been succeeded by a second, and a third and more numerous generation of black clergymen so that blacks were not only dependent on whites for the Christian gospel any more even though white people might think so. Separate black churches-mainly Baptist due to the congregation independence of that denomination-sprang up not only in the North where emancipation allowed blacks to organize institutionally but also in the South where any kind of black autonomy was regarded as subversive by the entrenched slave system. In the North and upper South two black evangelical denominations formed and selected their own bishops to lead them. Black American missionaries also established Baptist and Methodist congregations in Nova Scota, Jamaica and Sierra Leone (Raboteau, 1987, p. 92).Thus blacks took a leading role in the spread of Christian gospel and evangelical religion. Blacks also made evangelical Christianity their own by assuming leadership in their own religious life. By doing so they denied that Christianity was a white religion.

The opportunity for black religious separatism resulted from the egalitarian character of evangelicalism. The egalitarian tendency of evangelical revivals had been one of the major attractions to black converts in the first place. Racial and social status was overturned in the Baptist and Methodist societies in the 1780s and 1790s. Runaway slave advertisements in Virginia and Maryland newspapers complained that blacks were being ruined by the leveling doctrines of Baptists and Methodist evangelicals. It was not surprising that Anglican authorities in Virginia and North Carolina jailed evangelical preachers and mobs frequently harassed or assaulted them (Isaac, 1974, pp. 318-353).

Blacks were impressed by this gospel of freedom and after white Evangelicals retreated from the antislavery principles and became more respectable, they acknowledged that Christianity and slavery were contradictory. In the North it was possible for blacks to criticize slaveholding Christianity publicly; in the South the message had to be muted, whether their critiques were open or secret. By 1800 black Evangelicals won a significant victory of the war to assert their manhood. By that date the black church began. (Raboteau, 1987, p. 93; Raboteau, 2000)

Because they converted, churched, and pastured themselves, black Evangelicals were able to deny in effect that Christianity was a white religion. Even in the South where whites were legally in control of congregations, their control was nominal since black exhorts and deacons functioned in reality as the pastors of their people. At times black evangelical congregations challenged white authorities and in some cases succeeded in preserving their independence from white domination as did the African Methodists of mother Bethel in Philadelphia and the black Baptists of First African in Savannah. The astute leadership of men like Richard Allen and Andrew Marshall was tangible proof of black competence and skill in the affairs of men (Brooks, 1922, pp. 172-175). The power of black preachers in the affairs of God was symbolically even more valuable.

2. Compensatory and Transcendent

As seen in Chapter IV, many African Americans adopted evangelical Christianity during the revivals of the eighteenth and nineteenth centuries. Then how could the Christian God be loved by African Americans while they were suffering under slavery? While racism undermined the slaves' sense of worth as black people and reinforced their dependence on white masters the inward conversion of revivalism reshaped the individual slave's view of himself and of the world."The eyes of my mind were open, and I saw things as I never did before." One recalled his conversion experience. "Everything looked new," another said (Raboteau, 1987, p. 100). The visionary experiences moved the slave through a series of emotional transformation from fear to security, from pressure to release, from depression to elation and from sorrow to joy.

In the narrative of his life, Federick Douglass said that moment of internal transformation confirmed him that he was free even though stilled enslaved. Conversion "experientially" convinced the slave's value as a human, not a beast for labor and his ultimate worth as one of the chosen of God no matter what white people thought.[4]

Blacks could accept Christianity because they rejected the white version with slavery. It was God in African-American

---

4 http : //www.toptags.com/aama/books/book10.htm

religion who responded to blacks' prater and led to righteousness. According to Mays, Blacks were sure that god never forgave slavery and that he would end it: the problem was how and when. They also believed that the issue was ultimately in God's hands (Raboteau, 1987, p. 100; Raboteau, 2000).

The belief that God would liberate them was embedded in the vast majority of spirituals. According to Higginson, the spirituals emphasized the Old Testament and the exploits of the Hebrew Children. It is important that Daniel, David, Joshua, Jonah, Moses and Noah were delivered in this world and delivered in ways which struck the imagination of the slaves. There songs continually focused on the spectacle of the Red Sea opening to allow the Hebrew slaves to pass before inundating the mighty armies of the Pharaoh. They delightedly imagined the image of little David defeating the great Goliath with a stone. Over and over they told the stories of the blind and humbled Samson destroying the mansions of his conquerors; of the ridiculed Noah patiently building the ark which would deliver him from the doom of a mocking world; of the timid Jonah attaining freedom from his confinement through faith (Cohn & Hyon, 1987, pp. 56-57).

As mentioned above, African-American identity was based on the biblical story of Israel's enslavement and Exodus from Egypt. The Exodus story was the most important myth for black slave identity. White Americans had always regarded themselves as Israelites in Canaan, the Promised Land. Black Americans were Israelites in Egypt. Nevertheless, they thought of themselves as a chosen people destined for some special task under the direct protection of God. Identification with Israel was strengthened during the emotional climaxes of the prayer meetings. Slaves dramatically reenacted the events of the Bible in their worship, and the congregation became the biblical heroes in their imagination whom they sang, danced and preached about (Raboteau, 1994, p. 6).

The image of the chosen people was contained in many slave songs. Thousands of the spirituals identified the singers as "de people dat is born of God," "we are the people of God," "we are de people of de Lord," "I really do believe I'm a child of God," "I'm a child of God wid my soul sot free," "I'm born of God," "I'm a child of God wid my soul sot free," "I born of God, I know I am." There is no doubt that "to the promised land I'm bound to go," "I walk de heavenly road." (Levine, 1977, p. 69)

The force of this image could not be decreased by the observation that similar images were present in the white evangelical songs during the first half of the nineteenth century. White Americans could sing of triumph and salvation given their longstanding heritage of the idea of a chosen people which was strengthened by the belief in inevitable progress and manifest destiny, and the spread-eagle oratory. However, it was different and more significant that a chosen people was expressed by Negro slaves who were told endlessly that they were members of the lowliest of races. The images of the chosen people offered an insight into the kinds of weapons the black slaves had to prevent the internalization of the stereotyped images their masters consciously and unconsciously foisted upon the slaves (Raboteau, 1987; Raboteau, 1994, p. 8).

For the blacks, songs of God and the mythic heroes of their religion were not confined to any specific time or place, but were suitable to almost every situation. The religious historian Mircea Eliade has maintained that for men in traditional societies religion is a means of extending the world spatially upward so that communication with the other world becomes ritually possible and extending it temporally backward so that the paradigmatic acts of the gods and mythical ancestors can be continually reenacted and indefinitely recoverable. By creating sacred time and space, blacks could perpetually live in the presence of his gods, could surely believe that within his own lifetime "rebirth" was continually possible and can impose order on the chaos of the universe. According to Eliade "life is lived on a two-fold plane; it takes its course as human existence and at the same time shares in a trans-human life, that of the cosmos or the gods (Eliade, 1961, p. 4).

This notion of transcendence reached the essence of slave religion and through them the essence of the slave's world view. Unable to achieve an adjustment to the external world which involved meaningful forms of personal integration, attainment of status and feelings of individual worth that all human beings long for and need, the slaves created a new worth by transcending their narrow confines where they were forced to live. They extended the boundaries of their restrictive world backward until it fused with the world of the Old Testament and upward until it became one with the world beyond. Thus blacks could survive by internally creating an expanded and transcendant universe.

The God the slaves sang of was not remote and abstract but as intimate and personal as the gods of Africa had been. "O When I talk I talk wid God," "Mass Jesus Is my bosom friend," "I'm going to walk with {talk with, live with, see} king Jesus by myself, by myself," were refrains that echoed through the spirituals.

In de morin, where I rise
Tell my Jesus, huddy Oh,
I wash my hanes in de morin' glory
Tell my jesushuddy Oh.
(Allen et al., 1951, p. 47)

The heroes of the scriptures- "sister Mary" "Brudder Jonah," "Brudder Moses," "Brudder Daniel." were also similarly intimate (Levine, 1977, pp. 73-74).

As well illustrated in spirituals it was not the masters and mistresses but God and Jesus and the entire Old Testament figures who set the standards, established the precedents and defined the values. The world of the slave songs was a black world in which no reference was ever made to any white contemporaries. The slave's positive reference group was entirely made up of his own peers: his mother, father, sister, brother, uncles, aunts, preacher fellow "sinners" and "mourners" of whom he sang endlessly, to whom he sent messages via the dying and with whom he was reunited joyfully in the next world (Levine, 1977, pp. 73-75).

The transcendent nature is nowhere better illustrated than in the slave's visions of the future, which were a direct negation of his present. Over and over, the slaves sang of reaching out beyond the world that confined them, of seeing Jesus "in de wilderness," of praying "in de lonesome valley," of breathing in the freedom of the mountain peaks:

> Did yo' ever
> Stan' on mountun
> Wash you'han's
> In a cloud?
> (Allen et al., 1951, pp. 30-31).

They also held out the possibility of imminent rebirth :"I look at de worl' an' de wrol' look new··· I took at my hands an' they look so too··· I look at my feet, my feet was too" (Allen et al., 1951, pp. 128-129). Thus black Christianity as a compensatory religion enabled black people to believe that God never forgave slavery, and encouraged them to accept their lot as the will of God. Besides, for them religion never constituted a simple escape from this world because their conception of the world was more expansive than modern man's.

3. Social and Political

Is Black Christianity characterized as only a transcendent and compensatory religion? The answer is of course No. The African American Christianity has another nature: social and political. Black minister was present in his community's daily activities preaching funerals, weddings, prayer meetings, and Sabbath sermons with a force that uplifted blacks and proved the ability of black men. So, racists in the North and South found it necessary to slander black churches and black preachers by ridicule and restriction in order to be consistent with the doctrine of white supremacy (Lincoln, 1974; Lincoln & Mamiya, 1990; Raboteau, 1987).

Milton Sernett (2000) claims that scholars from the 1960s and 1970s onward, influenced by the Civil Rights movement and the rise of a new black nationalism, emphasized the historic protest strain. Although otherworldliness could be compensatory, it is not directly related to inaction in this life. African American slaves made the Christian afterlife their own and formed their understandings of it in subversive ways. They retained their African traditions in which the now and afterlife were not separate as white preachers argued. They laced their spirituals with double-meanings, for instance, freedom in heaven and a desire for freedom in the present. They also looked forward to a future reversal of the situations where they would prosper and their masters suffer. According to Emily Burke (1986), a white New Hamshire native who taught in Georgia during the 1840s, the slaves believe that in the life to come there will also be white people and black people, and then the white people will be slaves, and they shall have the dominion over them. The African American slaves believe that the weak triumph over the strong, and the poor win over the rich, and ironic reversal could provide oppressed peoples with a belief in ultimate justice and an ability to see themselves having the last laugh (Lockley, 2004).

Since the African American church was established in 1774 as the center of social, economic, spiritual and political growth, however, there has been support on its potential for political movement (Callhoun-Brown, 2001). Historically, black churches have been related to politics because of slavery and segregation (Lincoln & Mamiya, 1990; Nelsen & Nelsen, 1975). Because African Americans were discriminated against participating in American Mainstream institutions the church became the channel for all of social activity in the black community (Frazier, 1964). It can be said that the

African American church was one of the first independent institutions organized by Africans in the Americas during and after slavery (Gadzekpo, 2001; Lincoln & Mamiya, 1990). The church has been the center for religious practices as well as social and political activity.

The racial hierarchy was threatened by independent exercise of black authority, even though spiritual in nature. Whites had tried to confine Christian egalitarianism to the spiritual. The boundary between the spiritual and temporal equality was too frequently blurred. However, despite the threat to slave control that black religious independence posed, could be possible. To deny blacks the possibility of preaching or gathering for religious meetings would have encroached the tradition of gospel freedom action. When legislators took this action, evangelical objections caused to amend or evade the law. (Raboteau, 1987, p. 94; Raboteau, 2000).

Thus black churches were as much more than asylums from the spirit of slavery. As Bishop Daniel Alexander Payne of the A.M.E. church put it, in the African Methodist and Baptist churches they "found freedom of thought, freedom of speech, freedom of action, freedom for the development of a true Christian manhood" with the exercise of freedoms that may sound like civil and political rights. The black evangelical ethos asserted "manhood" rights which were considered a vital form of self governance. In this sense long before emancipation, the black evangelical churches were political. In the

North the free black churches functioned as political institution not only because black Evangelicals connected the concept of "Christian manhood" with the exercise of political rights (Payne, 1954, pp. 1-3).

Black Evangelicals believed that their duty was to act. Three movements formed the arenas for black organization and activism in the North-anti-slavery, anti-colonization and moral reform. Emphasizing solidarity with their slave brothers, Northern black clergymen many of whom were refugees from the south organized antislavery societies; "agitated from pulpit press and platform against slavery and oppression"; encouraged boycotts of slave-produced goods ; formed networks to help runaway slaves ; and strongly objected to the American Colonization Society's Plan to repatriate Afro-American in Africa (Raboteau, 1987, pp. 99-102; Sernett, 1975). In these causes they tried to answer the question, "what must we do to end slavery". Through they believed the final outcome was in God' hands, this belief did not lead them to fatalism or quietism.

In the South, slaves also strongly believed that God would save them from bondage as he had done the biblical children of Israel. Indeed their situation was appropriately depicted in Moses' words to the Israelites at the Red Sea: "Stand still and see the salvation of God." Former slaves said that Christianity did foster Quietism as well as acts of resistance, something claiming both in the same slave. External acts must be distinguished from internal attitudes, especially in a situation like American slavery where coercion and effective police power made rebellion futile in many cases. "External accommodation did not necessarily entail internal acceptance. Oppression may easily force outward acquiescence but internal dissent is virtually impossible to control" (Raboteau, 1987, pp. 99-102; Sernett, 1975). The inner world of slaves was the fundamental battleground and there evangelicalism worked as an important weapon in defending psychological, emotional and moral freedom of the slaves in white-dominated world. Evangelical Christianity helped slaves resist oppression and brutalization, as well.

Long after emancipation, William Herald, a former slave in Georgia reflected that he had first learned the meaning of manhood from William White, a black Baptist preacher from Augusta who came to Heard's country town to deliver apolitical address shortly after slavery. The seventeen-year-old Heard was so impressed by a White's speech that he decided "from that night to be a MAN and to fill an important place in life's arena." He was even more impressed when White accomplished his tasks as agent for the Freedman's Bureau, editor of the Georgia Baptist and organizer for the Republican party without fear, despite threats from local white democrats. The political activism of black evangelical preachers like Heard, Richard Cain, Henry, McNeal, Tuner, James W. hood, T.G. Campbell and others was a logical extension of the tradition of black evangelicalism (Heard, 1924, pp. 80-90).

Social and political nature which was embedded in the black evangelicalism was also well depicted in the black spirituals According to John Lovell, spirituals were fundamentally social and political. It was the spirituals which reflected the slaves' reality and well indicated that inhumanity was deeply rooted in the slavery. The spirituals also showed social consciousness with which slaves refused the oppression and restriction. Lovell also asserted that black Christianity not only helped the slaves transcend the suffering reality but also take a critical view of their masters, and to reject the ideological rationales for their own enslavement.

Since their inspiration was drawn from the events of the Old Testament and the Book of Revelation, the slaves continually sang of wars, battles, the Army of the Lord, soldiers of the Cross, trumpets calling the faithful and destroying the hosts of evil. These songs especially were "available for camp purpose." We'll cross de mighty river," his troops sang while marching or rowing.

We'll cross de danger water….
O Pharaoh's army drownded!
My army cross over.

"O blow your trumpet, Gabriel," they sang

O Blow your trumpet louder;

And I want dat trumpet to blow me home
To my new Jerusalem.
(Parrish, 1942, p. 247)

Black Union soldiers found it appropriate to accompany their fight for freedom with their sacred songs. Thus their religion was of this world as well as the next (Levine, 1977, pp. 70-80).

Although Jesus was ubiquitous in the spirituals, it was not the Jesus of the New Testament but a Jesus, an Old Testament warrior: "Mass Jesus" who engaged in personal combat with the devil; "King Jesus" seated on a milk-white horse with sword and shield in hand. "Ride on, King Jesus," "Ride on, Conquering King," "The God I serve is a man of war," the slaves sang. (Levine, 1977, pp. 79-80; Parrish, 1942)

There was always a latent and symbolic element of protest in the spirituals which often became overt and explicit. Frederick Douglass said that for him and many of his fellow slaves, the song, "Canaan, sweet Canaan/ I am bound for the land of Canaan," symbolized "something more than a hope of reaching heaven. We meant to reach the North and the North was our Canaan," and he wrote that the lines of another spiritual, "Run to Jesus shun the danger, / I don't expect to stay much longer here," had a double meaning which included the thought of escaping from slavery. Similar meaning was embedded when the black troops in Higginson(1870)'s regiment sang:

> We'll soon be free, [three times]
> When de Lord will call us home
> (Parrish, 1942, p. 247)

Slaves used their songs as a means of secret communication. An ex-slave told Lydia Parrish that when he and his fellow slaves "suspicioned" that one of their members was "telling tales to" the driver, they would sing lines like the following while working in the field:

> O Judas he wuza'ceitful man
> He went betray a mos'innocen'man
> Fo' thirty pieces a silver dat it wuz done
> He went in de woods an'e' self he hung
> (Parrish, 1942, pp. 247-248).

Thus, the black church, while giving spiritual freedom, has been involved in significant movements for social and political freedom (Mitchell, 2004). African Americans were not allowed to organize for fear of insurrection and rebellion by their white slave owners before the Emancipation Proclamation in 1863 (Meshack, 1976). There was the outlawing of African ritual dancing, complex drumming codes as communication and medical practices (Mitchell, 2004). White

Christians tried to persuade blacks to believe that slavery was a divinely-sanctioned institution and that eternal salvation would be a slave's reward for obedience. But even with exposing slaves to their own religious practices, whites became increasingly antagonistic because of fear of conspiracy. Slavery and segregation limiting the freedoms of African Americans made black denominations eventually formed and established separately from their white counterparts (Calhoun-Brown, 1996; Sherkat & Ellision, 1991).

4. African Heritage

4.1 Shouts and spirits

Although there are many African peoples possessing different cultures, traditions, customs, and languages in the vast continent of Africa, they share in common the importance of religion. In African societies, religion is an integral part of the lives of the individuals, the community as a whole, and the family. Religion is a way of life as well for African peoples. Moreover, the essence of Christian life for blacks was not ethics but liturgy. Ecstatic behavior, in the form of spirit possession, was central to the liturgy of slave evangelicals. Commonly the rites of worship consist of drumming the rhythms of the gods, singing their songs, creating a setting for them to come down and "ride" their devotees in states of possession. The possessed assumed the personality of the god, danced his steps, spoke his words, bore his emblems, and acted out his character in facial expression and gesture. (Raboteau, 1997, p. 7; Raboteau, 2000; Sernett, 1975).

Slaves found tangible relief from the misery of slavery in the ecstatic worship of the praise meetings. Former slave vividly remembered the scene: "They'd preach and pray and sing-shout too. I heard them get up with a powerful force of the spirit, clapping' they hands and walking' round the place. They'd shout, "I got the glory… in my soul.' I seen some powerful figurations of the spirit in them day."This kinds of meetings encouraged participants to include references to individual misfortunes and problems in their prayers and songs, which might be shared by all (Raboteau, 1987, p. 101).

Slaves and their descendants engaged in a type of ecstatic behavior called shouting. Shouting usually occurred at the frontier camp meetings. Whereas several accounts of these meetings focused on the slaves shouting, white revivalists also shouted and jerked, barked and laughed a holy laughter. However, according to Herskovits, the participants at Negro revivals were more active than white congregations; "greater rhythm and spontaneity" were characteristic of the black revivalists; the black preacher's sermon was more melodic, less halting than the white minister's. Besides, he asserted that the differences between white and black congregations in the manifestation of ecstasy were derived from the differences between the worship character of African and European cultures (Southern, 1991, p. 25).

In 1807 Jesse Lee, a Georgia evangelist noted:

> The first day of the meeting, we had a gentle and comfortable moving of the spirit of the Lord among us; and at night it was much more powerful than before, and the meeting was kept up all night without intermission. However, before day the white people retired, and the meeting was continued by the black people (Raboteau, 1980, pp. 316-317).

The slaves expressed religious emotion in certain types of bodily movement more than the white masters. Blacks sought and welcomed the presence of the Spirit, which led people to shout and dance not only during the special "seasons of revival" but also during regular church services. When Frederick Law Olmsted visited a black church in New Orleans he encountered the power of evangelical preaching to arouse ecstatic behavior.

> …. He soon began to respond aloud to the sentiments of the preacher, in such words as these : "Oh, yes!" and similar expressions could be heard from all parts of the house whenever the speaker's voice was unusually solemn, or his language and manner eloquent or excited Sometimes the outcries and responses were not confined to ejaculations of this kind, but shouts, and groans, terrific shrieks and indescribable ex-

pressions of ecstasy-of pleasure or agony-and even stamping, jumping, and clapping of hands were added (Olmsted, 1986, pp. 310-311).

In terms of theological interpretation and meaning, African sprit possession was different from the shouting experience of the revivalist tradition. However, in the context of action, the patterns of motor behavior resulting in or from the ecstatic experience, was derived from African forms of sprit possession. Hand-clapping, foot-tapping, rhythmic preaching, call and response, singing, and dancing are the behaviors related to possession both in Africa and in the U.S. The strong concentration on rhythmic preaching, singing, moving and dancing in the religious behavior of the American slaves has long been noted by observers. Ex-slave Robert Anderson depicted religious behaviors which he saw in his youth during slavery:

> The colored people … have a peculiar music of their own, which is largely a process of rhythm, rather than written music. Their music is largely, or was … a sort of rhythmical chant. It had to do largely with religion and the words adopted to their quaint melodies were largely of a religious nature. … The stories of the Bible were placed into words that would fit the music already used by the colored people while singing these songs, the singers and the entire congregation kept time to the music by the swaying of their bodies or by the patting of the foot or hand. Practically all of their songs were accompanied by

> a motion of some kind··· the weird and mysterious music of the religious ceremonies moved old and young alike in a frenzy of religious fervor··· We also had religious dances, which were expressions of the weird, the fantastic, the mysterious, that was felt in all our religious ceremonies (Anderson, 1979, pp. 24-26).

The original religious songs of blacks were distinguished from the standard Protestant hyms that they sang. In addition, black patterns of behavior influenced white revivalists at the camp meetings. Christian evangelist John Watson complained about the musical behavior of black revivalists in the Philadelphia conference:

> ···the evil is only occasionally condemned and the example has already visibly affected the religious manners of some whites. From this cause, I have known in some camp meetings from so to 60 people crowd into one test, after the public devotions had closed, and their continue the whole night, singing tune after tune, ··· scarce one of which were in our hymn books. Some of these from their nature, (having very long repetition choruses and short craps of matter) are actually composed as sung and are almost endless (Raboteau, 1980, pp. 28-31).

While evangelical missionaries forbade people to dance as sinful, they allowed slaves sacralized type of dancing "in the emotionally charged setting of the revival". The religious dance which was most frequently depicted was the "ring shout", or the circle dance. The ring shout is a ritual combination of music and movement that was widely recognized and practiced during slavery. Although much less common now, it is still present in the more limited form of "holy dance" and individual "shouting" in many of the most traditional Black church congregations. It was a ceremonial activity created by people in many different parts of west and central Africa who found themselves together in a difficult new land and were faced with the need to remember traditions that could enable them to survive here (Harding, 2007, p. 269).

The ring shout was a particularly strong example of African-influenced dance style in the U.S. The ring shout was a widespread and deeply ingrained practice among slaves (Southern, 1991, p. 25). The following passage from A.M.E. Bishop Daniel Alexander Payne's autobiography implies that he had seen the ring shout in many places a little over a decade after slavery:

> Pastor said: "Sinners won't get converted unless there is a ring." Said I: "you might sing till you fell down dead, and you would fail to convert a single sinner, because nothing, but the spirit of god and the word of God can convert sinners." He replied: "The spirit of God woks upon people in different ways. At camp-meeting there must be a ring here, a ring there, a ring over yonder, or sinners will not get converted." This way his idea and it is also that of many others. Theses "Bands", I have

> had to encounter in many places···To the most thoughtful··· I usually succeeded in making the "Band" disgusting; but by the ignorant masses··· it was regarded as the essence of religion (Payne, 1969, p. 253).

African slaves felt most free to sing spirituals accompanied by the ring shout dances when they were away from the gaze of slave holders and when the slave quarters were far enough away from the residence of masters. Black people might gather there in one of the cabins, moving to the side the meager furnishings so that a danced circle could form in the center of the room. The narratives of former slaves mention that a large tin basin was sometimes overturned and lessen the likelihood that the gathering would be discovered. Or, the basin or barrel might be filled with water and set in the middle of the room or by the door in the belief that it could serve a similar purpose of dampening down the sound. When slaves had access to their churches, with moveable benches or pews, the ring shout ceremonies often occurred there, after the formal "sermon" service was completed. People often gathered in woods bordering the plantations where they lived or in simply constructed "praise houses" or "hush harbors" or sometimes out in the open air, around a fire. There they would raise up the song and move in an easy, slightly weighted step in a counterclockwise ring, starting with a slow tempo and gradually building to a cadence that featured the syncopation of handclaps, feet stomping and percussive sticks to keep and vary the rhythm. And in the repetition of the sung lines and the movement of the circling bodies, the spirit was called and answered (Harding 2007, p. 270).

Dancing was a crucial part of worship for blacks. There were close parallels between the style of dancing observed in African worship and the style of the American "ring shout." Folklorists John and Alan Lomax who recorded a ring shout in Louisiana in 1934 explained the parallels:

> We have seen "Shouts" in Louisiana, in Texas, in Georgia and Bahamas; we have seen vaudou dancing in Haiti ; we have read accounts of similar rites in works upon Negro life in other parts of the Western Hemisphere. All share basic similarities; The song is "danced" with the whole body, with hads feet, belly and hip; (2) the worship is basically a dancing-singing phenomenon; (3) the dancers always move counter-clockwise around the ring; (4) the song has the leader-chorus form, with much repetition, with a focus on rhythm rather than on melody, that is, with a form that invites and ultimately enforces cooperative group activity; (5) the song continues to be repeated from sometimes more than an hour, steadily increasing in intensity and gradually accelerating, until a sort of mass hypnosis ensues … This shout pattern is demonstrably West African in origin.
>
> (Lomark & Lomax, 1947, p. 335).

As Harold Courlander said, "Circular movement, shuffling steps and stamping, posture and gestures, the manner of standing, the way the arms are held out for balance or pressed against the sides the movements of the shoulders, all are African in conception and derivation" Lorenzo Dow Turner asserted that the very word "shout" derived from saur a ter, used by West African Muslims meaning "dancing or moving around the Kaaba." (Raboteau, 1980, p. 71).

If as Payne (1969) said, the "ignorant masses" thought of the ring shout "as the essence of religion" and if the shout leader's argument that "without a ring sinners won't get converted" represented general belief, the "holy dance" of the shout may have played a significant role of connecting the core of West African religions-spirit possession-to the core of evangelical Protestantism-conversion experience. In the slaves' minds, the process of conversion may have had something to do with the African-style period of initiation into the cults of the gods. Slaves commonly spoke of the period of seeking conversion as "mourning" and regarded it as a time when the sinner should leave home alone to go to a quiet place to fight with his sins.

Thus, in the ring shout and similar patterns of ecstatic behavior such as anthems, and jubilees which served different occasions and reflected different moods, the African heritage of dance was expressed in the evangelical religion of the American slaves. Similar patterns of response- rhythmic clapping, ring, dancing, singing all of which preceded and followed the state of "possession trance"-showed the slaves'

African religious background. The revival camp meetings, where enthusiastic and ecstatic religious behavior was encouraged, provided a good settings for slaves to combine African patterns of response with Christian interpretations of the experience of spirit possession. The protestant revivalist tradition accepted by blacks proved in this instance to receive the influence of African styles of behavior. In spite of their prohibition of dancing as sinful the slaves reinterpreted and "sanctified" their African tradition of dance in the "shout". While blacks danced under the impulse of the spirit of a "new" God, Christian God. They danced in ways their African ancestors could have recognized (Raboteau, 1980, p. 72; Sernett, 1975). The styles of spirituals ranged from the exciting tempo and rhythmic stamp of the shout to the slow, draggy "sorrow songs" which usually passed through mind when the spirituals are mentioned. Even though the lyrics and themes of the spirituals were derived from biblical verses affected by the sacred and secular songs of whites, the way and the style in which the slaves sang the spirituals was African.

Though the singing style of the slaves was African, the spirituals or ring shout were performed to praise the Christian God in America. The names and words of the African gods were replaced by Christian God and biblical figures. African Americans used their homes, wooded and isolated places, and structures they built for sheltering or their gatherings to meet, to dance, to sing and to thus call spirit into their minds.

African style and European hymns met, which created new Afro-American song and dance to express the joys and sorrows of the new religion which the slaves had made their own.

4.2 Spirituals

Along with ring shouts shown in section 4.1, the spirituals tend to draw primarily on the Hebrew Joshua fighting the battle of Jericho to derive a sense of power, purpose, and identification in the present in contrast to the attention paid by white Protestant hymns to the Old and New Testaments. James Weldon Johnson was intrigued by the fact that the birth of Jesus appears to have held little interest for the poets of the spirituals, unlike the creators of many white Protestant hymns (See Levine, 1977; Raboteau, 2000; Ramey, 2002).

The focus on the Old Testament in the spirituals may also be attributed to the overwhelming importance of the Exodus to the black American slaves. Raboteau (2000) regards the Exodus as a primary symbol of differentiation between the white slave masters' Christianity and that of the slaves. For the African settlers explored and claimed their Promised Land of Israel in the form of America, a religious pact was fulfilled on the shores of their new home. However, for the African slaves America was not considered Israel, but rather Egypt, that is, the place of bondage and alienation that removed them from their destiny.

The writers of the spirituals clung to a historical precedent that offered Black slaves hope in the present and for the future. The African American slaves believed that God would act in the world once again to free them too. God's ability to intervene in the present would have been a perspective shared by nineteenth-century blacks and whites alike, but the slaves would obviously have sought a direct and aggressive action. In many of the spirituals, the Promised Land, the North was demonstrated by the slave poets to activate selectively varying features of the belief systems at hand to convey constructively their message (Beringer et al., 1986).

Black slaves espoused heaven in the spirituals as the release and reward of the true believer, although the spirituals reflect a combination of elements of African, Old Testament, and New Testament influences. The image of heaven is typically quite an earthly construction: not materially different from an idealized vision of life on earth, reminiscent of imagery of mobility and simple physical pleasures. Heaven is home, a potent symbol to those who were largely born into slavery, had hardly the potential to own anything, and were separated from family members and the geographical and ancestral roots so crucial to African culture. In addition, for the African slaves, heaven as home is a place that could only exist in the imagination and its inhabitants are blessed with a wealth of earthly physical and emotional comforts, and freedom (See Raboteau, 1987, 2000).

The spirituals also draw on African tropes and symbols. Satan is often described as a fraud figure. For African slaves, time is integrally linked to events and experiences, which are then related to one another regardless of differences in chronology or space, as if metaphysics were suspended. The spirituals seem to be an African cultural legacy in combination with the Christian teachings and their own interpretations of the texts. Therefore, the spirituals have the feature of creative metaphorical blends. The poets of the spirituals illustrate an mysterious conceptual ability to build images and metaphors that enable them to virtually move through the Old and New testament.

According to John Mbiti (1970), the African slaves think of the future as a direct and almost immediate extension of the present moment, with past and present as the dominant states of consciousness. In terms of the Christianity embedded in the spirituals, this conceptual orientation of African culture would certainly influence notions of future reward as well as the omnipresence of past occurrences. An African legacy shown in the spirituals is related to intimate and personal bonds which are maintained among individuals even after death. Besides, the African heritage depicted in the spirituals is expressed in an ability to reach into the heavens and touch ancestors and biblical figures alike as in the case of Exodus.

In the spirituals we can readily see the intimate connection between individuals and their social group. The spirituals certainly reflect the shared communal living and working environment of the slaves in their transplanted American culture, that is, a communalism that also reflects African values.

The spirituals embody a permeable boundary between the sacred and secular or an intimate relationship between these two realms of experience. This is consistent with poetic tradition yet has rarely been demonstrated with such power and poignancy. The spirituals should be classified as lyric poetry, whose theological value is directly related to their literary and cultural significance.

Spirituals are one of the most ancient and definitional of literary devices, speaking directly to such central operation as irony, metaphor, and allusion. Precisely what makes the spirituals most uniquely African is what aligns them to literary tradition and removes them from the category of folksongs.

The spirituals link together sacred and secular imagery with an ease how closely these two worlds-if they even were separate spheres were connected for their creators. By means of biblical imagery these poets are able to forge an intimate connection with other times, places, and characters through the sheer vitality of their belief in such a way that all of time and space seem coextensive. Their inherited African perspective would have made them particularly comfortable with this worldview. Their circumstances as slaves in the American South might have made it a necessity. The Old and New Testaments offered them the content and context (Ramey,

2002).

The spirituals are often regarded as carrying "coded messages" conceived by the Blacks who sang them but not necessarily by slave holders. Spirituals such as "Wade in the Water," "Go Down Moses," and "Follow the Drinking Gourd," served unsuspected purposes of alerting slaves that an opportunity to escape was near. Other spirituals, like "Run, Mary, Run" and "Oh Freedom" which respectively included the lines "You got a right to the tree of life" and "Before I be a slave, I'll be buried in my grave" provided courage to resist slavery by both internal and external means (Harding 2007, p. 276; Stewart, 1997).

In addition to these kinds of codes, there is a substrata of cipher in the spirituals that highlights yet another connection to sister traditions of the Afro-Atlantic diaspora. This level of "secret language" was present in the sound of the songs, the way they were sung: the elided tones and repetitions, the humming, the broomstick and stomped feet percussive accompaniments; the chants, the prayers and responsive callings in entrancing rhythm. These distinctive elements of traditional spirituals were echoes and adaptations of African forms of communicating with the divinities and the ancestors. In this sense, the songs were not only codes for freedom and courage, they were also codes for summoning the spirits of Africa, in the ancestral ways (Harding 2007, p. 277; Stewart, 1997).

Like a great deal of poetry, spirituals demonstrate a high

level of cognitive freedom: they are not conceptually bound by truth constraints, which accounts for much of their particularity and beauty. The poets of the spirituals had freedom wherever they could, which is an example of the unshackled state of mind. They were able to achieve freedom in their writing under circumstances of unimaginable restraint. Let us focus on one spiritual in particular, "Oh Mary., Don't you Weep, Don't you Moan," which is typical in some ways. What appears below is a composite version, which contains the verses that most commonly appear in various collections:

> Oh Mary, Don't you weep, Don't you Moan
> Oh Mary, Don't you weep, Don't you Moan
> Oh Mary, Don't you weep, Don't you Moan
> Pharaoh's army got drownded
> Oh Mary, don't you weep.
>
> One of dese mornings, bright and fair,
> Take my wings and cleave de air,
> Pharaoh' army got drownded,
> Oh Mary, don't you weep.
>
> I thinks every day an I wish I could
> Stan on de rock whar Moses stood
> Pharaoh's army got drownded,
> Oh Mary don't you weep
>
> I thinks every day an I wih I could,

Stan on de rock whar Moses stood,
Pharaoh's army got drownded
Oh Mary don't you weep.

One of dese mornings, round 5 o'clock.
Di sol world gonna reel and rock,
Pharaoh's army got drownded,
Oh Mary, don't you weep.
Don't know what my mother wants to stay here fuh,
DUs ikewirldain't been no friend to huh,
Pharaoh's army got drownded,
Oh Mary, don't you weep.
(Ramey, 2002, p. 357)

In the five stanzas above, we can see analogies everywhere, most notably in the refrain "Oh Mary, don't you weep, don't you moan/Pharaoh's army got drownded," in which the two situations-from Hebrew and Christian Scriptures are not apparently similar. The analogies appear in every verse, as three states remained in these five verses: "there is the political and legal state of being free on earth; heaven as the site of release from earthly bondage-a doubly resonant symbol for slaves who were Christians and by means of references to the Exodus tradition, the state of anticipation of release from bondage to freedom on earth, by means of identification with Moses and the Israelites." (Paris, 1995; Ramey, 2002, p. 357)

The spirituals express a view that is explicitly Christian in depicting heaven as the final home of the true believer and represent belief in Jesus as the means of reaching the final destination, home. For slaves, the theological implications of death are incorporated with particular passion as a desirable substitute to the life that they are leading. The freedom of the afterlife is consistently associated with imagery of release from bondage on earth. Strong message of political revolt is embedded in the spirituals with biblical principles of ethical conduct and the slaves' perception of the hypocrisy of the Christian teachings (Paris, 1995; Stewart, 1997; Ramey, 2002).

It is the Exodus tradition that maintains their faith and appears to form a direct parallel to their immediate situation of being another chosen people in a state of enslavement. The Promised Land is a multivalent symbol: "it is the reward, building on the Exodus tradition, for their faith; it represents freedom on earth, whether a return to African or the abstract condition of freedom as a state and concept; often used to refer to the North, a place of escape and deliverance that specifically represented freedom within the social and historical context of the African American slave poets; and it is heaven in Christian terms. It is also the Exodus tradition that allows them to apply Hebrew Scriptures themes to their literal and immediate political frame, believing without doubt that they would be freed on earth by God through their unwavering belief." (Paris, 1995; Stewart, 1997; Ramey, 2002, p. 358)

The first stanza of "Oh Mary, don't you weep, don't you moan" speaks from the person's present to one time frame in the past while referring to another. The speaker directly addresses Mary who appears in the frame of the Christian Scriptures, soothing her by telling her to remember another past of the Hebrew Scriptures which is the past in relation to Mary as well as the poet. At the same time the speaker refers to a past that is implied to be alive for them both. Likewise, three literary spaces including the poem itself and three chronological periods are invoked in dialogue with one another in the first stanza, which also forms the refrain typical of the spirituals (Benett, 1995; Ramey, 2002, pp. 358-359).

The second stanza reflects an imagined future in the person's life-time, in order to be read as taking place both in the persona's future and in an imagination. This is portrayed by means of conventionalized imagery of metaphorical flight in the form of birds, feathers, leaves and may be read as referring to both flight through death and freedom on earth. The third stanza, even though it is not strictly prophetic, still builds on a prophetic tradition in its combination with wishful projection and belief in the possibility of deliverance on the Hebrew Scriptures model. This stanza provides the poem's most explicit statement of identification of the poet with Moses and the Hebrew slaves, envisioning a desired future by means of the example of the past (Benett, 1995; Stewart, 1997; Ramey, 2002).

The fourth stanza explicitly repeats revelation in its prediction of a future turmoil that the whole world will experience. The final stanza represents the immediate present by referring to the personal frame of the person's mother. This stanza also forms an apparent ironic contradiction to the refrain or response, giving suspicion on the persona's emphatic statement of belief. How does the refrain, "Oh Mary, don't you weep, don't you moan, / Pharaoh's army got drowned" apply to Mary? The slaves wish to be freed to enter the Promised Land, and therefore refer simultaneously to a return home to Africa, the state of freedom in itself, and heaven. On the contrary, Mary is not a slave and does not anticipate being freed, as did the people of Israel under Pharaoh's control in the metaphorical invocation of the Exodus tradition or as did the African Americans under slavery in the metaphorical reference to freedom (Benett, 1995; Ramey, 2002, pp. 359-360).

There are a similar blending of chronological and conceptual realms in countless spirituals, including "City called heaven", "Motherless Child" "Nobody know da trouble I see", "He never said a Mublin' word", "I know Moonrise", "steal away", "I got a Home in Dat Rock." (Ramey, 2002, pp. 360-361). The metaphorical blends integrate realms that cannot be physically joined, and make a figural representation of the ability of the slave poets to transcend physical constraint by creative and imaginative means.

The spirituals were special but representative of the adversities that African Americans have overcome. They are clearly lyric poems that are sufficiently literary and unique to be considered a vital complement to the American poetry canon. Thus, the spirituals are an embodiment of the merging of the aesthetic and devotional in African American religion and culture. This familiarity with God, rooted in African understandings of relationship between human beings and the divine, seems to have had unique characteristics in America. In the experience of slavery and the consequent struggles of resistance, there seems to have been a greater need for the presence and protection of sacred spirits.

4.3 Magic and Supernatural

Thus far, we have discussed how new found Christianity and African traditions merged harmoniously into a creative and unique African American religion. However, there exist contradictory spiritual beliefs between African traditions and Christianity. In other words, conjuration and Voodoo beliefs about wandering souls and guardian spirits directly opposed the monotheism espoused by the church.

Chireau (2006) claims that the dissonance and convergence between African traditions and Christianity have been experienced as a single unit within the African American cultural experience. According to Chireau (2006), magic coexisted with Christianity as an alternative means to communicate with the spirits. She suggests that these seemingly divergent traditions have worked together in a complicated, compensatory fashion to provide spiritual empowerment for slaves.

Sharla Fett (2002) offers a more detailed description of African American healing practices, such as herbalism, conjuring, and midwifery, and describes how they became arts of resistance in the antebellum South. She argues that while white slave-owners narrowly defined slave health in terms of soundness for labor, slaves believed that health was intimately tied to religion and community. African American healing practices functioned to nurse the body and worked as a tactic of rebellion against whites. Fett (2002) found that the revered role of female root workers in plantation health cultures gave them authority and status within enslaved communities. As a result, power struggles arose between slave doctoring women and the white plantation owners. By examining the dynamics of plantation healing, Fett shed new light on the hierarchy of power in antebellum American slavery (Raboteau, 2004).

The most prevalent theme associated with slave culture's understanding of the supernatural was the belief in the existence of flying spirits who interfered in the lives of humans. Slave society focused on a *High God* who was deemed the supreme creator of the world and all forms found in it. Slaves held that this God was believed to be too important to meddle in the affairs of man. Instead, the slaves believed that spirits, with their capability of flight, monitored the matters of the world and thus directly impacted everyday lives. This understanding of one true god and his lesser spirits was derived from the West African religious belief in an omnipresent being that transcended ritual relationships with humans.

Wiliam Bosman, a Dutch slave trader who documented his experience with the Atlantic slave Trade described the beliefs of the Africans he encountered, "It is certain that they believe a god created the universe, and therefore vastly prefer him before their idol gods. But yet they do not pray to him or offer any sacrifices… god they say is too high exalted above us, and too great to think of Mankind; wherefore he commits the government of their world to their spirits." Enslaved people believed that the spirits were capable of animating objects in nature to affect the welfare of the people and so it is imperative to maintain good relations through dutiful praise, sacrifice and obedience (Murray, 2007).

The most significant form of flying spirits found in slave's perception of the supernatural was a witch. Witches were believed to cause illness or death simply by eating an individual's soul. Many stories featured the spirit of the witch taking on an animal form in order to fly to gatherings where the spirits of other witches congregated to consume a soul. If the animal was killed when possessed by a witch's spirit, the sleeping body of the witch was to die at the same instant. Witches were predominantly female, but they affected both genders for a variety of reasons including lust, revenge, and jealousy. Possession by witches was widely used to explain and justify a sudden change in behavior. Black slaves believed that you could save someone from a witch's spell by sprinkling salt and pepper on the presumed skin of the invisible witch's form; this act would prevent the witch's re-entry into her body. This belief came from the widely circulated folktale called *Wee Winnie Witchy* (Chestnut, 2008; Chireau, 2006).

Ghosts were another form of flying spirits that held a significant position in impacting the daily activities of Southern plantation life. In his journal, runaway slave William Grines describes ghosts as common as pig tracks. However ghosts were not considered evil or dangerous but regarded more as cunning and sly tricksters. Ghosts were sometimes portrayed as schemers who played tricks on unsuspecting humans. Ghosts were understood as spirits of the deceased who returned to haunt the living as an imposing nuisance. Some stories discuss the ghosts of cruel masters, who returned from the grave to continue the torment of their slaves. In his autobiography former slave Lewis Clarke recalls "I was actually as much afraid of my master when dead, as I was when he was alive." Slaves used tactics such as burying a corpse face down to prevent its return from the grave, placing a broom at the front door to keep ghosts from entering and scattering mustard seeds on the floor of a room to confine the ghosts. These references to ghost proofing demonstrate the spiritual aura that slaves believed ghosts possessed (Chestnut, 2008; Chireau, 2006; Shea, 1984).

Ancestors were another powerful class of spirits included in slaves' paranormal beliefs. References to revered ancestors, who died long ago or those of more recent memory, abound in the diverse forms of slave culture documentation. If a person neglected the veneration of their ancestors, they would be at risk for sickness, misfortune and even death. Thus, ancestors played a role of watchful guardians for the customs of the people and would invoke punishments if anyone, particularly their kinsmen, deviated. As a result of these strong convictions, a large part of slave culture was centered on the spirits of the ancestors. There is an obligatory worship between man and his ancestors, emphasizing burial rituals in slave society. Improper or incomplete funeral rites can interfere with or delay the entrance of the deceased into the spiritual world and may cause his or her soul to linger about restless and malevolent places. Before a funeral was complete, several customs must be observed including proper preparation of the body, ritual mourning after burial, and strict rules about varying levels of mourning (Mcnamara, 2010).

As mentioned thus far, witches, ancestors and ghosts are vital to understanding slave's perception of the world of spirits, but it is their participation in the art of conjure that most links their beliefs about supernaturalism to their everyday lives. Conjuration was a magical tradition in which spiritual power was invoked for various purposes such as healing, protection, desire and self-preservation. It has the means by which the slaves communicate with and manipulate these spirits they so ardently believe. While magic possessed multiple functions in slaves community, its most salient had to do with practices of racial opposition. The signification of conjuration as a deterrent against slave owner oppression is ubiquitous in slave narratives, personal testimonies, interviews and especially folklore (Shea, 1984).

African American magic exists all around us today. It resounds in contemporary exhibitions of Voodoo in New Orleans, the rituals at African-American religious services and in lively artistic forms throughout our museums. Thus, we should understand African American beliefs concerning the supernatural and where these beliefs originate. Folklore, narratives, autobiographies and interviews have much to say about what magic has meant to the African slaves and forged a distinctive culture. Because of their experience of compulsory bondage and racial persecution, their perception of magic differed greatly from their European American counterparts. The understanding of the supernatural world would be necessary and helpful in perceiving escaped and espoused notions of spirituals empowerment to black slaves.

5. Slave religion and archeology

The archaeological understanding of New World slavery as a social institution begins with the concept of 'ethnicity'. The issue of ethnic identification in archaeology is not new any more. Childe (1926) stated several decades ago that the correlation of cultural with racial groups is generally hazardous and speculative and beset with pitfalls. The agreement between the archaeological past and the ethnographic or historical present is seen as a close or near-perfect match. In many cases, an historical archaeologist may be excavating a site for which an abundant documentary record exists. The archaeological understanding of ethnicity is very significant in historical archaeology in general. As a way in which to study ethnicity and the contacts between ethnic groups, New World historical archaeologists have turned to the study of slavery. In addition, slavery has relevance outside the narrow confines of scholarship. The understanding of this social institution appeals not only to professional anthropologists and historians but also to thousands of non-scholars in society at large (Orser, 1990, 1991, 1994).

According to Frazier (1964), embedded within the archaeology of slavery is the once much-debated question of whether the Africans, who were enslaved and brought to the New World, had their cultures destroyed by the Middle Passage, the horrendous trip across the Atlantic Ocean. These enslaved and traumatized Africans had their cultures literally ripped from them. In this vein, the social landscape of the New world was truly a new one. Orser (1994) claimed that the slaves' trauma was also carried over into religion because the horrors of slavery caused their traditional religions to collapse. Any expression of an African belief in the New World was simply a vague memory rather than part of a living cultural tradition.

The current most prevalent view, however, contains two central propositions: that Africans did not abandon or lose their cultures during enslavement and the Middle Passage, and that the cultures they forged in the New World were not exact duplications of those in Africa. Through interactions with diverse Africans, Europeans, and Native Americans, enslaved Africans created a syncretic culture in the New World (Orser, 1991, 1994).

Slave religion is an exceedingly complex and multifaceted subject. Although manifestations of African religions appeared in the New World in varying degrees, it seems logical to assume that each has archaeological correlates. We may further assume that the material expressions of slave religion included both places of worship and associated religion objects. It may be easy to imagine the contextual union of these elements. We may easily associate places of worship with hymnals, candle sticks, crosses, books and other readily identifiable pieces of religious material culture. For clandestine slave religion practices, we can understandably envision the difficulty in associating religious places with religion objects.

The problem with such identification is well voiced by Mrs. Channel, who lived on a plantation where the conduct of religious ceremonies by slaves was expressly forbidden: the slaves would steal away into the woods at night and hold services. They would form a circle on their knees around the speaker who would also be on his knees (Cade, 1935, p. 331). One clear object of such religious service beyond worship is secrecy. In these clandestine religious observances, we can expect little in the way of easy association between place and object. The religious places selected by slaves seeking to conduct traditional rituals were hidden and the artifacts used for their religious observances were everyday things pressed into service.

Many of the powerful religious objects slaves made in the New World seem to have to do with magic. As seen in section 4.3, magic is an interactive religious belief system wherein spells can be cast and warded off, where the future can be foretold and where the sick can be healed. Historical archaeologists who search for evidence of slave religion look for material culture easily associated with religious magic because only in the rarest of contexts such as magic can traditional religious items be clearly related to slaves (Orser, 1991, 1994).

At Newton Plantation, a seventh-century sugar estate on the island of Barbados, Handler & Lange (1978) found the remains of an old man of African descent which they named 'Burial 72'. This individual had been buried with several commonplace objects such as copper bracelets, white metal rings and a metal knife. Most interesting objects were an elaborate necklace and a baked clay smoking pipe that had also been placed alongside this deceased man. The necklace contained seven cowrie shells, twenty-one drilled dog canines, fourteen glass beads of various sizes and colors, drilled vertebrae from a large fish, and one large carnelian bead (Handler & Lange 1978, pp. 125-132; Handler et al., 1979)

A Christianized African burial was discovered a few years later at the first official cemetery in New Orleans, Louisiana. The Catholic fathers of this French colonial settlement on the banks of the lower Mississippi River sanctified this burial ground sometime before 1722, and later deconsecrated it in 1788. The French inhabitants of the city removed their ancestor's remains for reburial elsewhere. At the very bottom of the social hierarchy were enslaved Africans. Archaeologists excavated thirty-two of these interments as part of a rescue project (Orser et al., 1986; Owsley et al., 1985). Only one of the still solid cypress caskets contained any religious objects. These objects are a rosary with 63 black wooden beads and two silver medals (one emblazoned with St Christopher, the other with the Madonna and Child) and a glass and white metal medallion with the image of the Virgin Mary etched in gold on the glass face. These items were found with Burial

11.

Ferguson (1992) conducted detailed and innovative study of several Colono Ware vessels found in South Carolina and Virginia. He claimed that many of the otherwise mundane, shallow bowls in this tradition were incised on the bottom with an 'x' an 'x' enclosed in a circle, or an 'x' with arms extending outward like a reverse swastika (Ferguson, 1992, pp. 110-16). These marks appeared to represent identification symbols placed on the pots by their makers. Potters throughout eighteenth-century Europe used similar marks on their ceramic wares (Kovel & Kovel, 1953, p. 213) and an 'x' is an easy mark to make in wet clay.

The idea that the X's on the case of Colono Ware vessels may represent maker's marks is plausible, (Orser, 1991, 1994) but Ferguson (1992) offers a much more intriguing interpretation. He interprets these crosses, X's as symbols of an African cosmology, because they are often found on the interior base of the vessels rather than on the outside, as is true of most makers' marks and sometimes resembling the encircled cross of the Bakongo sign of the cosmos (Thompson, 1983, p. 109). The bakongo-a populous people living in today's Zaire-used earthen pots to contain powerful substances associated with healing and the control of the supernatural (Thomson 1983). Among the Bakongo, the association of pots with healing extends all the way to Ne Kongo, the renowned founder of their culture. Based on this ethnographic evidence,

Ferguson (1992, p. 115) asserted that South Carolina's marked bowls were made and used by American descendants of the mythical Ne Kongo who cooked medicines in earthenware pots. In addition, these pots because of their obvious difference from European glazed wares also served as a form of unconscious resistance to slavery and the plantation system (Ferguson, 1991, p. 37). These clay pots were a way for slaves to proclaim their traditional cultures in an nonvocalized and relatively nonthreatening manner. The etching of powerful religious symbols on the insides of pots was another way for slaves to retain a piece of African in the New World.

Historical archaeologists overlooked the scratched 'X' marks for years due to the mundane character of the earthenware pots. These lines were often interpreted to be cut marks made by knives (see Ferguson, 1992). The common appearance of the pots and the nagging uncertainty over exactly who produced them, among native Americans, slaves, or creoles obscured the issue of how they were used for religious observances, and clouded whether they had a religious function at all. Therefore, there needs to be much further research on Colono Ware before a definitive statement of its meanings can be presented.

Objects that may be recognized as religious in nature are the small, brass, fist-shaped amulets found at the Hermitage, the early nineteenth century Tennessee plantation home of United States President Andrew Jackson. To date, archaeologists have found three fists amulets in the slave cabin deposits of the Hermitage. Since the temporal context of these objects is in the antebellum period, before the American Civil War, their association with slaves is certain. The fists are small in size and are made of a stamped copper alloy, two of which clench rings and their third fist incorporates a hook (Orser, 1991, 1994).

The fists from the Hermitage are not exactly like *figas*. A true *figa* has the thumb extending upward between the first and the second finger in a symbolic representation of a cross. The example from Santa Elena is true to this form (South, 1991, p. 72), but the fists from The Hermitage lack the finger and thumb arrangement and are simply in the form of clenched fists.

Both the marked earthenware pottery vessels and the brass fist amulets seem to reflect something about slaves belief systems. The meaning of either class of artifacts, however, is ambiguous. The pottery marks may be just maker's marks. The fists may be simple souvenirs with no deeper significance. Nonetheless an interpretation that makes reference to slave religion and belief system is not only appealing, but it also adds a substantial new dimension to our understanding of African-American slave life (Orser, 1991, 1994).

The archaeology of slave religion has not had a long history. However, the archaeology of slave religion is meaningful in the search for answers to significant questions in their religious lives of slaves such as slave diet, social relations and material elements of resistance. Through the archaeology of African American religion, we could examine the religious lives of the African men and women who toiled on the plantations and within the cities of the plantation world. In this regard, the archaeology of slavery is such a rapidly growing field. It is also likely that we will know appreciably more about slave life and religion than we do now.

The biases that exist in the present data might be derived from archaeologists' preoccupation with large plantations. The reasons for this emphasis on the very large estates of the wealthy lower South and Carribbean are varied, but typically they relate to founding and local interest. It has generally been easier to obtain scarce funding for plantation archaeology when a historically important person is associated with the property. For this reason, active archaeological programs have been conducted at plantations associated with Andrew Jackson, George Washington and Thomas Jefferson and with together notable members of the elite planter class (see Orser, 1990).

In the Unites States, the largest estates are typically among the Atlantic coast. Much of this focus has been driven, not by the research design of archaeologists but by the needs of land developers. This prized real estate was also valued in the past by the wealthiest planters, and therefore, the sites that have been studied, usually under the requirements of preservation legislation, have been also the large coastal estates. Federal bureaucrats have easily been able to judge these large estates with their famous owners, to be significant and worthy of federally funded study (Orser, 1990, 1994).

Historically, however, most plantations are not large. The typical plantation in the American South was small in acreage, housed less than ten slaves and was cultivated by the master working alongside the slaves (Stamp, 1956, pp. 30-31). These kinds of plantations formed the backbone of the American slave system. Nonetheless, it is only within the past year or so that archaeologists have turned their attention to these small unimpressive estates (Andrews & Young, 1992).

In terms of religious beliefs the distinctions between large and small plantations are significant. A former slave in Mississippi said that "we didn't hear nothing 'bout hants [haunts] or charms". It was on the big places where all such as that went on (Rawick, 1977c, p. 219). This comment signifies that the size of the plantation may have played a role in whether and how slaves were able to express their religious beliefs. It can be assumed that slaves on larger estates had more anonymity and could have more easily maintained elements of a traditional religion than slaves on small plantation farms.

Nonetheless, the intriguing idea that plantation size and religious tradition is closely related cannot be addressed at this time. Archaeologists studying slave religion are still too few in number, and our collective knowledge is too fragmentary to make a conclusive statement on this matter. However, there is sufficient and good reason to believe that the study of slave religion along with slave life will continue to grow in its importance. Thanks to the study of archeology, eventually we will be able to write a more complete account of the religious beliefs and practices of the African men and women who were held in bondage in the New World (See Orser, 1994).

06

African American religion after emancipation

1. Postbellum black religion

For many African Americans, emancipation seemed to be the fulfillment of communal deliverance in the 'here-and-now'. Uses of redemption rhetoric to describe emancipation showed the extent to which emancipation represented the fulfillment of group deliverance from the hell of slavery, not only for the newly freed, but also for already free black intellectuals (Gin, 2010, p.210).

Black elites collected their energies during Reconstruction to evangelize and educate former slaves. They sought to give religion a practical bent focused on 'the here and now.' In some city churches, emphasis on the life to come did indeed wane after emancipation according to a 1903 study of *The Negro Church* edited by Du Bois. Emancipation represented a significant break with the past, but there were complicated challenges to the African Americans: escalating terror and violence in the South; the North's increasing absorption with its own industrial problems; the racial Republicans' failure to commit to land reform. Many blacks continued to draw on the radical potential of otherworldliness that had developed in the antebellum era to resist the physical, material and political oppression that still swept much of the South during Reconstruction (Du Bois, 1994, 2001; Gin, 2010).

Emancipation represented a significant break with the past, but there were escalating terror and violence in the South. The North also confronted its own industrial problems, and the radical Republicans' failure to commit to land reform, which challenged African Americans' hopes. The political compromise between Democrats and Republicans that concluded Reconstruction in 1877 caused Southern freedom virtually to be abandoned by the North as reunion became a more critical objective for white politicians than racial equality (Foner, 1955). Many blacks continued to draw on the radical potential of other-worldliness that had developed in the antebellum era to resist the physical, material and political oppression that still swept much of the South during Reconstruction (Gin, 2010).

Even after emancipation, religion was not only a response

to oppression but also another resistance strategy in black and white relations of domination. We should understand more than the context of domination to recreate the otherworldly imaginations of post-war blacks and to understand the internal differences in the post-war African American community. Religion was about not only between themselves and external oppressors but also the relationships between themselves and God. Although they shared basic beliefs in God's ultimate ability to correct all wrongs and they believed that each group was not in itself homogeneous, black intellectuals and ex-slaves were also precipitous in different social and religion environment (Foner, 1955, Gin 2010).

Many black intellectuals were aware of the intrusions of science on the claims of religion, and of changing Protestant ideas that painted progress as the ultimate goal of existence. Ex-slaves, who still lived in the rural South, continued to draw strength from the power of suffering and endurance that some scholars suggest developed in the 'hell without fires' of slavery, even when they also took the concept of the afterlife to criticize the present social order and to suggest what meaningful freedom might look like (Gin, 2010, p. 212).

Ex-slave conversion narratives which were recorded in the late 1920s and compiled in the *God struck Me dead* collections enabled us to look at the varied religious imaginations of the newly freed. The richness of their visions illustrates the diversity of beliefs within the black community, loosely united by the themes of ultimate justice and communal salvation. Their narratives include many visions of heaven and hell drawn in a common pattern. The potential convert is first convinced of damnation and they believe themselves to be unworthy. Then they die and have out of body experience, going to hell before subsequently being redeemed and travelling to heaven. Finally upon coming out of the vision, the converts rejoice in their salvation and believe themselves born again (Gin, 2010, p. 213).

Cone (1970) had much to say about the afterlife. Cone could well have been one of the black intellectuals of the late nineteenth century, who complained about the overuse of the afterlife by ex-slave preachers, and wrote:

> We know all about pearly gates, golden streets and long white robes. We have sung songs about heaven until we were hoarse, but it did not change the present state or ease the pain… We want to know why cannot Harlem become Jerusalem and Chicago the Promised Land? What good are golden crowns, slippers, white robes or even eternal life, if it means that we have to turn our backs on the pain and suffering of our own children?
>
> (Cone, 1970, p. 241)

According to Cone (1970), the otherworldliness that African Americans saw in black Christianity meant a willingness to accept inequality and injustice rather than try to effect change in the here and now. All black visions of the after-life were not radical or political. For instance, the notion that the body would turn white in the other world, or in heaven, raised the black intellectuals dedicated to progress, and eager to inspire their people and implant a racially-biased pride.

However, otherworldliness may not be solely escapist and may not be purely otherworldly. For African slaves, imagining a future communal relief now and in the hereafter was a central way to endure and confront slavery and confirm their value as a people. Postbellum freedmen and black intellectuals retained traditions originating with slave religion and let them resound with the contexts in which they found themselves. For ex-slaves balancing their expectations for freedom with the disappointments by white restoration in the South, desire or hope for freedom and equality in heaven invoked a similar sense of strength and communal pride. Heaven itself provided a window through which they could envision what real freedom might look like: a 'piece ob land in glory', a house with 'vines on de poch', the ability to roam freely (Gin, 2010, p. 225).

For many intellectuals in the postbellum era, heaven was also about the freedom to envision, but of the mind through eternity, rather than the body through space, as they had the idea of eternal progress to encourage racial uplift. They also drew on the radical uses of otherworldliness that had developed under slavery to argue for the rights and equality of their people against whites who used Christianity to support their own supposed racial and cultural superiority. They truly believed that their idea of progress and justice in the here and hereafter matched better with their commitment to racial uplift, than the ex-slaves' material and emotional envision of the afterlife. Numerous visions of the afterlife, influenced by slave religion, affected access to mainstream Protestant trends, and complicated dynamics within the African American community, even as both groups used these beliefs to face the challenges of the late nineteenth century. The new freedmen or black intellectuals also did not consider the afterlife as merely illusory. However, they used the core concepts of ultimate justice, ironic reversal, and future bliss to make sense of the world where they lived. The slaves, freedmen and intellectuals all looked forward to the reversal of their status in the real world as well as in heaven.

2. African-American Religion and Food culture

We offer thanks to God for our sustenance and then share a meal. For many years in the black community that meal consisted of soul food-food that was lovingly prepared and designed to nourish our emotional, social and spiritual selves. We offer thanks to God for our sustenance and then share a meal. Our religious culture in a hush harbor or an urban church, reflected our gratitude to God for keeping us and nurturing our community.

Food and eating are consistent sources of imagery throughout the Bible beginning in Genesis and running throughout the text. Food is used as a tool for healing, an instrument in miracles and as a symbol of the body of Christ. Each instance highlighted the centrality of food to our religious and spiritual lives. These biblical references call our attention to the importance of our intake of the holy and use one of the most basic human functions, or eating, to reflect that our religion figuratively and literally nourished us (Hinton, 2008).

Eating is one of our most basic and important human functions. Given that "one of the earliest forms of security and of sensory pleasure is connected with the intake of food and that about it are centered the first human relations." (Powdermaker, 1997, p. 208), food has always provided more than mere nutrition. It provides early bonding with parental figures and numerous opportunities to gather with friends and family to share life's joys and woes. In many ways, black food rituals are borne from and reflect religious rituals as in the tightly proscribed Passover seder or the traditional Easter Lamb. Without question, food is integral to religion, similarly religion was once an integral component of black community.

Since religious life was black life and food is a central part of religion, food played a central role in the black community. The role of food in religion has been widely studied ranging from Sack's *Whitebread Protestants (*2000) perspective to analyzing the elaborate food rituals of early Christianity (Freeley-Harnik, 1994). Many non-Christian religions provide prescriptions that forbid certain foods, labeling them as unacceptable. The circumstance, practices, and traditions surrounding food is what holds the meaning for religious food rituals. Sack (2000) suggests that the actual food is important, not the substance which holds all of the meaning for food.

Food in the black religious tradition varies from that of other groups. "The essence of black culture has been handed down through oral history, generation after generation in the African tradition through the selection and preparation of soul food." (Hughes, 1997, p. 272). In the black community, unlike many others, the food itself carried as much meaning as the rituals and circumstances ascribed to the food.

Soler writes "cooking is a language through which a society expresses itself. For man knows that the food he ingests in order to live will become assimilated into his being, will become himself. There must be, therefore, a relationship between the idea he has formed of specific items of food and image he has of himself and his place in the universe. There is a link between a people's dietary habits and its perception of the world" (Soler, 1997, p. 55). The food that blacks were "given" by master was the lowest food forms: the cast-offs and unwanted entrails and appendages mirroring blacks' lowly status. However, the creativity, passion and love which were used to transform those meager offerings into a cuisine reflect the creativity, passion and love that African-American carried within themselves. Blacks did not become what they ate; they transformed what they ate into something better. It was the black family's ability to turn this food into "more" that gives the food stuff itself meaning. Blacks were given the leftovers. It makes the food important to black culture that these unwanted food could be transformed with our own hands, our own ideas and our own cooking skills. The food carried meaning, in and of itself.

It is also significant how foods were brought from Africa to the United States. In the early days of slavery, food provided a necessary link to a lost country and lost humanity. Yams, peanuts, okra, rice, and watermelons are a few of the foods that were brought directly over from Africa to the United States. As they were transported as seed, these foods carried great meaning. "Accessiblity to the roots of plants is preserved by possession of seeds. Forced to leave their native land, their home, family and African tribes, many slaves brought seeds with them." (Hughes, 1997, p. 272). This strategy maintained ethnic identity and food became an encyclopedia of black history and culture. Once again, in black culture the food had great meaning beyond it uses.

This does not imply that the circumstances of food and eating were unimportant in the black community. Food tradition and practice were varied and important. Food provided an opportunity to gather as a people. It represented freedom to explore and nourish one's own spirit, and to celebrate the relationship between family and community away from the watchful eye and oversight of the master. Food became a central element in religious ceremonies, allowing the enslaved to celebrate not only their God, but their humanity and community (Perdue, Brton & Phillips, 1976).

Food rituals offered a prophetic voice of hope and energy in the midst of empiricism, and these elaborate meals became a hallmark of the black community, taking on the name "soul food" which embraces the spiritual importance of the communal table and of eating. Powerful religious education took place during these food rituals, not only regarding the Christian story, but also by placing the Christian story in conversation with African-American communal history. This story was shared and handed down during these food gatherings (Hinton, 2008).

The significance of food has continued well into the 20th century when blacks were not allowed to eat in restaurants outside of their homes due to segregation laws and lack of access to restaurants (Hughes, 1997). The sharing of food became a survival mechanism as blacks participated in the great migration and needed to find respite in new surroundings. Food also became a signature of one's origins and a reminder of his or her home. For instance, though blacks left rural communities and were relocated to the urban north, a carefully prepared pulled pork barbecue dinner became a reminder of their North Carolina home.

Food and the attendant rituals taught blacks about self and community in relation to the divine. The meal became a source of religious education. The power and importance of food to religious practice, as important as in most traditions, were exponentially magnified in the black community. In the late 20th culture, where the civil rights movement brought some success and African Americans became economically and socially diverse, religious culture in the black community began to shift. (Hinton, 2008).

While it would be an overstatement to suggest that the black church had been faltering, it is clear that the late 20th century saw a significant shift in black church. For the first time since its inception there was a decrease in the involvement of young people in the church, and by the 1990's generation of unchurched black youth began to emerge (Lincoln & Mamiya, 1990). Further, as middle-class black churches began to imitate the worship practices of white churches, a religious schism between middle and lower income blacks increased. Even though membership roles did not decline precipitously the black church began to falter.

For the majority, leaving home in the 1970s also meant leaving their churches and the traditions and neighborhoods they were familiar with as children. The upward mobility, however, turned out to be a somewhat lonely journey. All middle and upper-class African Americans have not experienced the joy and fulfillment that they thought their economic achievements should have accompanied. They still needed the warmth and security of their homely black churches (Lutz, 2001, p. 97). The black church was no longer the center of identity for African-Americans. As mega churches emerged and personal spirituality began to take the place of religious culture, communal and symbolic elements in the black church diminished.

It is also important that religious education that placed the black experience in conversation with the Christian story began to disappear. People did not want to hear about the unending struggle and the metaphor of blacks as the new Israelites. Rather, they took solace in attending churches that spoke to the arrival of blacks. Instead of educating towards freedom and liberation in the black church, in many areas, African Americans began to educate themselves towards privatized religion and prosperity (Hinton, 2008).

The most troubling loss in African American religion was loss of the prophetic voice of the black church. Since its foundation in the 17th century, the black church had stood against injustice and employed its power of proclamation to rail against the status quo. This voice supported the black church and black people through nearly three hundred years of tortured existence and offered hope where there was none. This prophetic voice provided strong influence to a nation during the civil rights movement and was constantly heard from the black church.

However, the prophetic voice began to be lessened in the late 20th century. As a new gospel geared towards comfort statements and personal prosperity emerged, the prophetic voice began disappearing. As a community, African-Americans were beginning to reap some economic and social fruits of centuries of struggle, but this assimilation included the adoption of majority values of independence and privatization. As a community, it became easier for African-Americans to neglect those who have little and to focus on those who have much.

Given the relationship between food culture and religious culture, it is not surprising that concomitant with the loss of religious culture, African-American food culture in the US shifted in the 20th century. First, the communal and symbolic uses of food began to decline. If "food culture" creates solidarity, (Counihan & Van Esterik 1997, p. 1) then the solidarity of African-Americans was challenged in the late 20th century. Soul food was regarded as unhealthy and the cause of numerous health problems in the black community. Food became a battleground of health and social issues and no longer signified a gathering of community (Hinton, 2008, p. 5).

However, it may be reasonable to argue that it is the proliferation of fast and convenience food that have contributed mightily to the decline of health (increased diabetes, heart disease, obesity) in the U.S. in general and in the African-American community in particular (Dalton, 2006). As a targeted market of fast food outlets the African-American community under the same economic and time constraints of other groups, began to accede to the attraction of convenience foods (Dalton, 2006; Grier, 2005).

The African roots of soul food were surprisingly healthy. The use of fresh fruits, grains, nuts, and vegetables which were the primary sources of carbohydrates and protein in the African's diet, are what many now consider essential for a healthy lifestyle. Though the reasons were far from altruistic, the forced diet of the enslaved was one that maintained their health at top physical form (Perdue, Barden, & Phillips, 1976). That diet became soul food, the food that has recently been decried as unhealthy and a harbinger of poor health outcomes. The consistent and long-term movement away from this diet, the incorporation of more meat-based proteins, and the movement from careful preparation to fast preparation that caused a dramatic shift in the diets and health of African-Americans.

As African-Americans adopted a less than palatable (and less than healthy) diet, there were efforts to revive soul food. In the late 1960's entrepreneurs began exporting soul food to wealthy blacks in urban areas and the term "soul food" became a part of the common vernacular. In today's culture we see soul food restaurants increasing in popularity in Harlem,

NY with busloads of passengers-both black and white seeking an authentic soul food experience. Few patron mentions the irony of having to go out and buy what was once only suitable. Soul food is now considered a "treat"-something for a special occasion, not food to nourish the body and soul on a daily basis. Soul food, and the symbols and culture that once accompanied it, has been effectively divorced from our daily rituals and our souls (Hinton, 2008, p. 5).

Religious culture began to shift in the black community. Food culture also began to get lost in the black community. The losses occurred simultaneously and reflected a larger and more significant loss for African Americans. More privatized religion, more self-focus, more social gain, and more assimilation of the dominant perspective on the meaning of food ultimately yielded a communal and religious education loss over which we should all mourn. In order to return to the rich roots and traditions of the black community, soul food, the communal symbols of religion and food culture must be acknowledged and readopted by African-Americans (Hinton, 2008).

3. Religion and gender

This section will discuss the role of gender and religious authority in African American churches. African American church leaders long opposed to racial inequality but ironically, they willingly allied themselves with their former American oppressors in their pre-judicial subordination of women. A number of African American religious leaders appealed to the Holy Scriptures to justify the subordination of women, and continue to do similarly in their efforts to preserve male dominance over women in ecclesiastical contexts. The African American male church leaders deceive themselves into believing that they are justified by the Holy Scriptures (Paris, 2008, p. 482).

Some male-headed congregations explained that the lack of support for female clergy stemmed from their adherence to Biblical principles. They think that rejection of female religious authority was viewed as necessary to preserve the church's identity, and that not recognizing the legitimacy of female religious authority was not an issue of gender discrimination, but instead a necessary belief to preserve the truth as illustrated in the Word of God. However, not all congregations interpreted the Bible that way. Denomination also seemed to play a role in the acceptance of female clergy, with Baptists expressing the least support for female religious authority. Even among Baptist churches, there was openness to female religious authority because of the lack of male leadership. In a rural impoverished community, where the population is declining and men are given few opportunities to lead through employment and financial stability, there may be more supportive views about female clergy due to the lack of persons available to serve in a leadership capacity, even among denominations that do not recognize female religious authority (Levin & Taylor, 1993; Yeary, 2011, pp. 643-644).

Against this backdrop, African American women have raised their voices by forming their women's organizations and conventions with which to demonstrate their equality theologically, morally, and organizationally. The historian Evelyn Higginbotham concludes: Through the convention movement, black Baptist women established deliberative arena for addressing their own concerns. The largest black denomination in the world, however, the National Baptist Convention, U.S.A., Inc. and the fastest growing African American denominations in the nation, The Church of Godwin Christ, remain incurably patriarchal by excluding women from ordination. It is among the greatest of ironies that many African American women who are members of these churches fail to enjoy the equality within the churches that they experience daily in the secular world (Levin & Taylor, 1993; Paris, 2008, p. 483).

African American religious patriarchy is beyond understanding given the fact that more than two-thirds of black congregations are comprised of women. "Are so many of them brainwashed into thinking that patriarchal domination in the Black churches is different from patriarchy elsewhere? Why, then, do they go on giving the church their support and loyalty?" (Paris, 2008, p 484)

Yeary (2011) performed a case study of the role of gender and religious authority in African American churches located in a rural impoverished area through examining the personal characteristics of religious leaders, congregational views on female religious authority, and congregational culture. There were some similarities between female-headed and male-headed congregations: salvation message of Jesus Christ, perceptions of poverty and unemployment as significant community challenges. However, there were also some apparent differences. Female clergy tended to report a supernatural calling into ministry and more barriers than male clergy to lead a congregation, including more intensive preparatory training, a lack of mentors, and fewer opportunities to lead a congregation of their own. Given the great number of barriers faced by female clergy, a miraculous calling may have been needed for the female religious leaders of the area to accept their call into ministry. Gender discrimination also existed at the organizational level, with female-headed congregations reporting less access to resources to conduct church activities and non-acceptance by some segments of the community (Levin & Taylor, 1993; Yeary, 2011, p. 643).

On the contrary, in a rural, impoverished area characterized by racial discrimination, the church may be one of the few places left for Black males to be in power. Thus, protecting one of the last available domains for Black male leadership may be another reason why African American male pastors are less supportive of female clergy than white male pastors. Two distinct congregational cultures emerged from the data: Social Activist and Teach the Word. Both female-headed and male-headed congregations demonstrated aspects of both cultures, even though the Social Activist culture played a more dominant narrative in female-headed congregations compared to male-headed congregations.

Although all the congregations perceived the community's most challenging problems as social in nature, their response to the community's challenges differed markedly by their cultural orientation. Social Activist congregations saw it as their responsibility to meet the community's social needs and aimed to transform the community through providing social services through the power of Christ. Given the double oppression of race and gender faced by female-headed churches, a Social Activist culture may have been more salient to female-headed congregations. Teach the Word congregations stressed the importance of salvation, heaven, and knowing the Word of God, perhaps to emphasize what the community did have instead of what the community did not have to focus on what socio-economic circumstances could not take away (Yeary, 2011, pp. 644-645).

There is another group of people not affirmed by the African American churches whose God-given talents are highly visible and fundamentally important to the church's worship life. These are homosexuals, lesbians, bi-sexuals, and trans-gendered people whose God-given natures are not affirmed by the church and discriminated within the church. Since their sexual identities must remain invisible in the church, the church turns blind eyes to their pain and suffering caused by the widespread hostility that threatens their bodily security every day of the year (Paris, 2008).

4. Mega-churches and charismatic leadership

The African American church performs a myriad of functions within the African American community (Hill, 1997; Swain, 2008; Williamson & Kautz, 2009). It initially emerged as an "invisible institution," an informal network among the slaves which was instrumental for numerous endeavors among which were abolitionist activity and the Underground Railroad (Moore, 1991). The African American church continues to operate as a pseudo-family where congregants and nonmembers alike receive social support, avowal, and have the freedom to worship from cultural perspective (Johnson & Staples, 2005). Worship services are a vehicle for releasing stress, addressing disappointment from life's challenges. Through this worship services, African people can be encouraged to strive for economic, social, and political betterment.

The first formal African American church was established between 1750 and 1773 and was subsequently followed by the founding of others (Lincoln & Mamiya, 1990). These churches were responsible for the eventual formation of numerous African American institutions such as seminaries, black colleges, academies, insurance companies, and banks. By 1906, the African American church had grown to over 36,000 churches with a total membership of over 3.5 million people (Birchett, 1992). It is estimated that there are now between 65,000 and 75,000 African American churches with approximately three fourths of all African Americans holding church membership (Thomas et al., 1994; Hill, 1997).

Not only has the number of African American churches substantially grown but the congregational size has also burgeoned. Now known as mega churches, which boast memberships of 2,000 congregants or more, they are institutions that continue to be central to the African American community's spiritual, political, social, and economic activity and the means by which Blacks can relate to their Divinity through their cultural heritage. Because of the magnitude of the number of people who attend them and their vast economic resources, African American mega churches are in a strategic position to utilize their means to help alleviate a whole host of problems faced by the African American community (Moore, 2011).

These mega-churches have grown very rapidly in a very short period from small congregations of less than two hundred to three to five thousand. For the most part, the growth has occurred under the leadership of young, professionally educated charismatic clergymen. In other words, their personality and ministerial style attract large numbers of followers. The most important thing in these churches is the approval of the leader. In this regard, these mega-churches reflect a mark of the African American religious leadership which displays no sign of reduction. Charismatic leadership causes the initiatives of the laity to be meaningless by "making all the functions of its members auxiliaries to the leader's wishes." (Paris, 2008, p. 485)

However, it is reasonable to say that charismatic leadership is alive and well throughout the African American religious community, and these types of churches have been much more active in public life than other churches, mainly due to the leader's theological vision and his persistent demands for social transformation. For instance, Martin Luther King, Jr. leadership exhibited many marks of charismatic authority and charismatic leadership has contributed much more to the expansion of democracy in the nation.

Paris (2008) pointed out some of the inevitable problems

that result from charismatic authority are the following: (a) the organization's immense difficulty in choosing a successor subsequent to the death of its leader; an issue that is being resolved these days by many such leaders actually presiding over the process of selecting his/her successor; (b)the failure to develop strong leadership capable of independent thought, judgment, and action; (c)the resistance of independent-minded professional and academic élites to exchange rational discourse for charismatic authority; (d)the non-cooperative spirit of charismatic leaders in forming coalitions; (e)the proliferation of organizations and the duplication of resources which dissipate the power of the whole to effect substantive social change;(f) extravagant expenditure of monies for trivial purposes (Paris, 2008, p. 485).

Further, the new so-called "mega-churches" filled with thirty-and forty-year-old members thanking God for helping them gain access to corporate America, reflect the success model of corporate America. Their gradual acquisition of adjacent inner city properties coupled with their architectural designs exude a spirit of economic triumphalism which is both pleasing and problematic, depending upon how it is viewed. By analogy the pastor, as chief executive officer, is unquestionably at the helm of the corporation with various numbers of loyal subordinates carrying out his/her wishes and always working deferentially and loyally to gain their favor.

Since the African American pastor, by virtue of his/her ordination, is thought to be vested with special grace from the divine, his/her executive authority and status are considered greater than that of ordinary corporate executives due to their special relationship with divine authority. The pastor often reminds the people that his authority is deeply rooted in that divine source. Thus, loyalty to God and pastor is often not readily distinguishable. In other words, since the pastor is recognized as God's spokesperson in the proclamation of the gospel and the administration of the sacraments, it is often difficult to discern the difference between the pastors' will and God's will (Paris, 2008, p. 486).

Most important, since the clergy, by virtue of their ordination, are given authority on all matters pertaining to faith and morals, there remains little theological justification for the criticism of the laity. Those who recognize this fact and are disturbed by it, remain at a distance from the church's internal decision-making processes. More often than not, they are adherents but not active lay leaders. In large part, this accounts for the fact that less than one-third of the members of African American congregations are men.

There are numerous activities offered to the community by these churches such as self-help and a variety of support groups like those designed to benefit those who struggle with substance abuse issues and who have HIV and AIDS, lay health advisory networks, health coaching, physical fitness programs and gyms, youth development and after school academic tutorial assistance, latchkey programs, mental health counseling services, pastoral counseling, fatherhood initiatives, marriage, family and bereavement counseling, food and clothing outreach, nursing home and assisted living care, and a variety of other services that provide a context for empowering the African American community. Community empowerment "refers to the central and direct involvement of people in determining their own struggles, strengths and future" (Long et al., 2006, p. 18).

Further, being empowered is liberating because people then become involved in their own social construction and gain control over their own circumstances and future (Moore, 2011). These churches provide an ideal place for politicians and others to rally support for their causes. These African American clergy also become allied with the power elite in the irrespective communities. For instance, one such leader has served as the Secretary of State of New Jersey and another was appointed President of The State University of New York. (Paris, 2008, p. 487)

On the positive side these churches provide a home for countless numbers of people transplanted by the circumstances of their upward mobility in their economic pursuits. These churches provide a place where their personal, familial and spiritual needs are met, where their children can experience a rich environment for their spiritual and moral development, and where they can also find opportunities to serve others. Most important, every member feels that he or she is part of a very successful movement, which is very comforting psychologically

Further, these churches provide an ideal place for politicians and others to rally. To be sure, the total responsibility of helping our community does not depend solely on the shoulders of the church but given the resources that can be made available to the African American community through African American mega churches, we think that these institutions have the financial resources to make change not only on the individual but on the larger societal level to serve as a guiding light of hope in the wake of apathy, and most importantly, to foster community empowerment (Moore, 2011).

5. Religion, spirituality, and the African American Family

Religion and spirituality have always been important concepts to consider in understanding African American family life (Billingsley, 1992; Boyd-Franklin & Lockwood, 1999; Brashears & Roberts, 1996; Lincoln & Mamiya, 1990). Consideration of these concepts help to explain how African American families have historically used their faith and belief in God to assist them in dealing with the many adversities they have faced in being

Black in America (Billingsley, 1992; Lincoln & Mamiya, 1990).

This section reviews research that examines African American religion and spirituality. The following aspects of religion and spirituality will be explored: a) how the terms religion and spirituality are defined in the literature, b) who's religious, and c) the characteristics of religiosity and spirituality relevant to the African American family context (Wallace, 2009, p. 10).

The concept of religion has been utilized and understood in a variety of ways. Lincoln and Mamiya (1990) define religion as essentially a subjective experience. From their perspective, the experience is personal and viewed from the standpoint of the individual. Carlson, Kilpatrick, Becker, and Killer (2002, p. 157) define religion as "the formal institutional context for spiritual beliefs and practices." Here the understanding is that religion is the place where spiritual beliefs and practices can take shape. Lunn (2003) defines one's religiosity as being related to or manifesting faithful devotion to acknowledged ultimate reality. Mattis, Taylor, and Chatters (2000) define religiosity in terms of individual constructs: organizational, non-organizational, and subjective religiosity.

Organizational religiosity refers to behaviors that occur within a church context, mosque, or other religious setting. Such behaviors include church attendance, membership, or participation in church groups. Non-organizational religiosity utilizes religious practices that are tied more to a person's traditional understanding of the importance of their faith (Taylor, Mattis, & Chatters, 1999). Such behaviors occur outside of a formal religious setting (Taylor, et al., 1999). Non-organizational religiosity is less social in nature and instead emphasizes individual faith practices including private devotional practices, reading religious materials, watching or listening to religious programs, praying, and requesting prayer (Taylor & Chatters, 1991).

Subjective religiosity is defined as an attitudinal measure of religious involvement and is measured by such questions as perceived importance of religion, the role of religious beliefs in the individual's daily life, and the individual's perceptions of being religious (Chatters, Levin, & Taylor, 1992; Levin, 1997). McAdoo (1995) further defines subjective religiosity as a person's religious orientation.

Researchers have uncovered several predictors of who's religious and the amount of their religious participation within the African American context. Gender is the strongest and most consistent demographic predictor of religious participation (Levin & Taylor, 1993; Levin, Taylor & Chatters, 1995; Mattis, 2001; McAdoo, 1995; Taylor & Chatters, 1991). African American women are more religious and participate in religious activities more often than African American men (Levin & Taylor, 1993; Levin, et al, 1994; Mattis, 2001; McAdoo, 1995; Taylor & Chatters, 1991). Older African

American women are also reported to have higher levels of religious involvement (Levin, Taylor & Chatters, 2004; Mattis, 2001; McAdoo, 1995). Age, marital status, socio-economic status and regional differences are other additional considerations (Chatters, Levin, & Taylor, 1992; Levin, Taylor & Chatters, 2004; Mattis, 2001; McAdoo, 1995; Taylor, 1988b, 1986; Taylor & Chatters, 1991). Married individuals, for example, report higher levels of church attendance and membership (Taylor, 1988b, 1986), and African American individuals with higher socio-economic status are found to have higher levels of religious participation than their poorer and unmarried counterparts (Taylor & Chatters, 1991). Persons with higher levels of education and income are also more likely to be religiously affiliated. These demographic findings indicate that African Americans are diverse in their levels of religious involvement (Wallace, 2009, p. 12).

Characteristics of religiosity and spirituality consider how religious or spiritual individuals are, how often people attend religious services, what religious or spiritual activities individuals engage in, and how often they pray. Characteristics of religiosity and spirituality are also related to the function that religion and spirituality perform. Aspects of religiosity will be organized around the concepts of organizational, non-organizational, and subjective religiosity.

A large proportion of the African American community attends worship services on a regular basis. Based on the

National Survey of Black Americans and other national probability samples, about two-thirds of the African Americans report that they are church members. More than 40% report that they attend church at least once a week and 70% of African Americans indicate that they attend religious service a few times a month (Taylor et al., 2004). Elderly African Americans report higher levels of church attendance and participation than younger African Americans (Taylor, et al., 2004).

Non-organizational religiosity refers to behaviors that may involve private devotional practices, reading religious materials, watching or listening to religious programs, praying, and requesting prayer (Taylor, et. al., 1999). Prayer was found to be the primary activity in which African Americans engage (Johnson, Elbert-Avila, & Tulsky, 2005; Taylor & Chatters, 1991). Taylor and Chatters (1991) found that nine out of ten individuals indicated they prayed nearly every day. About 48% of those who never attended religious services also indicated that they prayed everyday (Taylor & Chatters, 1991). Older African Americans were found to pray on a more frequent basis than their younger counterparts, women prayed more than men, and widowed persons prayed less often than married respondents (Taylor & Chatters, 1991; Taylor, et al., 2004).

African Americans read religious material and listen to and view religious programs. Taylor et al. (2004) noted that 44%

of African Americans reported reading religious books on a daily basis. In one study, older persons with poor health were more likely to view and listen to religious programs than their healthier counterparts. African Americans with higher educational levels were less likely to engage in this activity (Taylor & Chatters, 1991). However, the relationship between educational levels and reading religious materials varied regionally. Chatters, Levin and Taylor (1992) found a positive association with southerners' levels of education and the reading of religious material. No relationship was found among respondents who resided in other regions. It was also found that no organizational behaviors were important outlets for religious expression for individuals in poor health (Taylor & Chatters, 1991; Wallace, 2009, P. 14)

Subjective religiosity is defined as the attitudinal measure of religious involvement (Levin, 1997). In the Taylor and Chatters' study (1991), a majority of African Americans still considered them religious whether or not they attended church. Taylor (1988) found that more than 40% of respondents who had no religious affiliation and over half of those who never attended religious services indicated that they were either very religious or fairly religious. Married respondents were found to demonstrate higher levels of subjective religiosity, as did women and older African Americans (Taylor, 1988b). African Americans also indicated that they would often seek spiritual comfort and support when confronted with problems regardless of whether they attended worship services (Taylor, Chatters, & Levin, 1995).

This was especially the case for individuals with lower income levels and for African Americans living in rural areas (Rosen, 1982). However, a more recent study (Mattis, Mitchell, Grayman, Zapata, & Taylor, 2007) found that this was not necessarily the case with requests for support from clergy such requests depended on the nature of the support needed.

Spirituality has also been understood in a variety of ways. According to Powell and colleagues (Powell, Shahabi & Thoresen, 2003), spirituality overlaps religion but is also distinctive from religion. Clemmons (1991) understands spirituality as the internal ongoing quest for self-knowledge that includes recognition of a higher power's presence. According to Kaut (2002), spirituality may be viewed as a "gestalt"- the summation of diverse aspects of life that collectively give meaning to one's existence (Wallace, 2009, P. 15). Spirituality enables healthy and active investment in life and provides the resources through which one can respond to infirmity, physical decline, and approaching death.

Spirituality also represents "the divine expression and belief of a higher power that governs one's existence" (Bowen- Reid Harrell, 2002, p. 21), and spirituality is regarded as an "individual's belief in the sacred and transcendent nature of life manifested in a sense of connectedness with others, humans, spirit, and God" (Mattis, 2000, p. 118).

From a theological perspective, Bridges (2001) defines spirituality as the foundation of African American culture, their religion, and their struggle for freedom. She suggests that spirituality informs African American world view - why African Americans do what they do. However, Paris (1995), another African American theologian, believes just the opposite. He believes that it is African Americans world view or cosmology that informs African Americans' spirituality. Therefore, studies with clear distinctions in the constructs are needed (Powell, et al, 2003, p. 50).

Research has shown that spirituality is important for the role that it plays in allowing people to experience connectedness (Pierce, 2001). Healthy spirituality results in a sense of belonging, acceptance, respect, well-being, and inner peace (Pierce, 2001). Research has also shown that African Americans' spirituality serves as a buffer between racism and stress-related health outcomes (Bowen-Reid & Harrell, 2002). African American women's spirituality, more specifically, "spiritual surrender" turning things over to a higher power assisted with African American women's meaning such as making and coping with life situations. This spiritual surrender required women to confront and relinquish their limitations. This spiritual surrender, however, enabled women to "gain the insight, protection and guidance needed to envision and achieve outcomes that they would not have been able to see or achieve on their own" (Mattis, 2001, p. 11).

Thus, regardless of whether individuals consider themselves religious or spiritual, both perform functions for individuals living their lives. Religious behaviors such as attending church, for example, provide means for informal social support. Regular church attendance encouraged meaningful social roles that provided a sense of self-worth and purpose through the act of helping. Non-involvement also excluded individuals from the traditional spiritual, social, and supportive functions of the church. Religiosity therefore appears to improve people's opportunity to receive support especially when they either attend church frequently or are official members of a congregation (Powell, 2003; Taylor & Chatters, 1988).

Spirituality plays an important role in connecting people. As a component of well-being based on values of commitment, love, and affection, spirituality is also believed to reduce the perceived stressful situations of caring and is an important reason given as to why, particularly with African American families, members assume the caring role (Peirce, 2001). Spirituality is composed of formal Christian beliefs and the secular value of care for one's own and suggests that one's spirituality is an important reason for African American family members' provision of care. (Archbold, 1995).

6. Contemporary African-American Worship Practices

Research on African-American worship suggests that ecstatic, participatory worship is unique to African-American congregations (DuBois, 2003; Lincoln & Mamiya, 1990; Mitchell, 1970; Park, 1944; Pitts, 1989, 1993). There are two worship practices most often examined in other work on ecstatic, participatory worship: verbal affirmation, also referred to as "call and response," and spontaneous physical worship (Mitchell, 1970; Nelson, 1996; Pitts, 1989, 1993). Verbal affirmation is here defined as the verbal responses of congregants employed to communicate approval of a sermon or other event during a worship service. Congregants declare their support with sayings like "Amen" or "Hallelujah" (Nelson, 1996; Pitts, 1989, 1993). Spontaneous physical worship is defined as an observable display of emotion and feeling among congregants demonstrated through physical manifestations including shouting, jumping, or dancing (Nelson, 1996; Pitts, 1989, 1993; Raboteau, 1978). Additionally, white congregations are used as a comparison group because white and African-American Christians share deep historical relations.

Some scholars suggest that verbal affirmation and spontaneous physical worship are reinterpreted, thinly veiled African religious rituals (Herskovits, 1970; Pitts, 1989, 1993; Raboteau,

1978), and contend that ecstatic, participatory worship is distinctly African American. DuBois (2003, p. 136) even argued that "the most characteristic expression of African character" is thought to be found among African-American congregations. In other words, ecstatic, participatory worship is linked to ethno cultural heritage, likely occurring in religious space where African Americans predominate. The rituals of colonial American Protestantism were amenable to the religious rituals Africans brought from their homeland. Given the constraints of slave life, Africans leveraged the religious ritual structures available to them as a means of retaining their culture and religious rituals. The contemporary rituals and practices reflecting African culture have been considerably modified. Nonetheless, evidence exists that African ritual behavior is sustained in African-American congregations in America today, although in new forms (Raboteau, 1978).

Worship services in some African-American churches are even structured to incorporate ecstatic, participatory worship (Nelson, 1996; Pitts, 1989). These worship practices are considered distinctive to African-American congregations. There are other religious practices thought to be specific to African-American congregations as well. These include the preaching style of African-American pastors (Mitchell, 1970; Pipes 1970; Stewart, 1997), the use of a syncopated drum rhythm during worship (Pitts, 1989, 1991), centrality of music to the religious rituals (Roberts, 1994), and the formal role of ushers (Nelson, 1996). Excluding preaching style, the research that has identified these religious practices as distinctively African American is limited (Edwards, 2009, p. 32). Nevertheless, we can assume that African-American congregations are more likely to participate in verbal affirmation or spontaneous physical worship than white congregations.

Others argue that contemporary African-American Christianity is a testament to early American revivalist religion (Marty, 1984). As Marty (1984, p. 110) puts it, "African-American Christianity is largely product of revivalist religion" Therefore, religious tradition explains African-American congregations' participation in ecstatic, participatory worship practices.

Revivalist religion has been central to the American religious system (Butler, 1990) and is credited with attracting and converting African Americans to Christianity (Pipes, 1970). The white revivalist ministers, whose success was far more dependent upon their effective use of very effusive, rousing preaching styles and messages of human depravity than formal religious education, tapped into the emotions of revival attendees (Marty, 1984). Converts, regardless of race/ethnicity, responded to their stylistic teachings with verbal affirmations, shouting, and other spontaneous physical worship expressions (Herskovits, 1970; Mitchell, 1970). According to this perspective, ecstatic, participatory worship is an innovation of enterprising white religious leaders that was used to incite and attract new believers. Whites' and African-Americans' participation in verbal affirmation and spontaneous physical worship during revival movements suggests that these practices are evident among contemporary white and African-American religious communities, particularly those with religious tradition trajectories rooted in revivalist religion.

Today's counterparts to the revivalist religion of past centuries are conservative Protestantism and African-American Protestantism. Compared to liberal Protestantism and Catholicism, the theology of contemporary conservative Protestantism is most consistent with revivalist religion, with its emphasis on evangelism, individual choice, and salvation (Marty, 1984; Warner, 1988). African-American Protestant denominations whose roots are also located in revivalist religion (Lincoln & Mamiya, 1990; Roof & McKinney, 1987) generally affirm the basic theological tenets of conservative Protestantism, and are historically known to emphasize social justice (Roof & McKinney, 1987; Steensland et al., 2000). Given that conservative Protestantism and African-American Protestant denominations have best sustained the spirit of revivalist religion, we would expect congregations in these religious traditions to be more likely than Catholic and liberal Protestant congregations to participate in verbal affirmation and spontaneous physical worship.

Although some have argued that African-American Christianity is a testament to revivalist religion, others consider Pentecostal religion to be the "heir of the frontier, enthusiastic-type. In a study of African-American Bostonian congregations, McRoberts (2003) found that while these congregations tended toward theological conservatism, they did not necessarily embrace a social or community justice agenda (Edwards, 2009, p. 34). In this regard, ecstatic, participatory worship is primarily a manifestation of Pentecostalism.

Pentecostalism, which began as an interracial religious movement during the first decade of the 20th century, has historically possessed a particularly strong emphasis on a personal, experiential, and emotional religion (Synan, 1971; Spittler, 1999). Pentecostal religion stressed the importance of tangible evidence of God's presence through speaking in tongues, healing, and other observable signs of God's involvement in both individuals' lives and, more broadly, congregational worship (Dayton, 1987; Nichol, 1971). So, while verbal affirmation and spontaneous physical worship were common in revivalist religion, these practices typified Pentecostalism.

Others claim that verbal affirmation and spontaneous physical worship reflects social class historically. For instance, those who have engaged in ecstatic, participatory worship have tended to be poorer and working class (Chaves, 2004). For this reason, some scholars have speculated that ecstatic, participatory worship is more a function of socioeconomic status than African origins or religious tradition (Daniel, 1942; Holt, 1940; Mays & Nicholson, 1933; Wilson & Clow,

1981). The less educated lower-class congregations tend to participate in ecstatic, participatory worship practices more frequently than more educated, higher-class congregations.

Lower-class congregations' greater participation in ecstatic, participatory worship is linked to a couple of explanations. Some researchers argue that the persistence of ecstatic, participatory worship among the lower class is a result of their need for emotional catharsis (Daniel, 1942; Pipes, 1970; Wilson & Clow, 1981). This religious expression is an accessible vehicle through which the lower-class person can emotionally release (Anderson, 1979; Holt, 1940; Pipes, 1970). An alternative explanation is that the higher classes refrain from ecstatic, participatory worships as a way of distinguishing themselves from the lower class (Drake & Cayton, 1970; DuBois, 2003; Harris, 1992; Pope, 1942).

Over the 19th century and into the 20th century, there was a movement toward a more formal, intellectual Christianity in America (Marty, 1984). Education increasingly became a qualification for ministry involvement. Intellectual religion was stressed among white denominations, leading to a decline in ecstatic, participatory religion and a rise in formal, uniform religion (Marty, 1984). A similar movement ran through African-American Christianity during the early 20th century. With an increase in these sentiments among religious intellectuals, the lines, whether real or perceived between religious practice and class status were drawn.

Many researchers who insist that revivalist religion is at the root of certain African-American worship practices have admitted that African culture is evident in African American worship practices. Nevertheless, they argue that these practices are the result of a merger of African culture and European religion rather than the reformation of African religious rituals under guise of Christian worship (Fauset, 1971; Pipes, 1970; Sernett, 1975; Stewart, 1997). In this regard, we can think that ecstatic, participatory worship is a mixture of ethno cultural practices and religious tradition.

Since African-American Christianity is rooted in revivalist religion, verbal affirmation and spontaneous physical worship may be most central to the religio-cultural repertoires of African-American congregations with revivalist religious trajectories. Therefore, ecstatic, participatory worship is particularly distinctive of African-American congregations affiliated with conservative Protestantism or African-American Protestant denominations.

This highlights the relationship between particular socio-demographic and religious characteristics of congregations and ecstatic, participatory worship. Placing these explanations within the theoretical frameworks of the cultural repertoire or religious marketplace, verbal affirmation and spontaneous physical worship can be seen as components of the cultural repertoires of African Americans or people of a certain class status that are used to foster a connection among group members. Verbal affirmation and spontaneous physical worship may be understood as resources used to increase the religious market share of a certain religious tradition or religious group. Thus, these ecstatic, participatory worship practices are core components of certain African-American religious groups' ethno cultural repertoires that facilitate their capacity to forge space within the religious marketplace (Edwards, 2009).

Previous studies on African-American worship practices, largely products of qualitative research with historical, anthropological, or theological emphases, have found that African-American congregations have participated in ecstatic, participatory worship from slavery through contemporary times (Drake & Cayton, 1970; DuBois, 2003; Herskovits, 1970; Pinn, 2002), generating widespread popular and academic perception that there are distinctively African-American worship practices. The rich, qualitative examples of African-American congregational worship provided in these studies give us an intricate, textured understanding of the religious context of ecstatic, participatory worship. The methodological approaches of these studies, however, do not establish whether or ecstatic, participatory worship is distinctive to the religiocultural repertoires of African-American congregations. In addition, they provide us with a comprehensive understanding of the factors associated with ecstatic, participatory worship in contemporary congregations.

Moreover, some research argues that factors other than ethno cultural heritage, like religious tradition, Pentecostalism, or social class, inform whether congregations' religiocultural repertoires will include ecstatic, participatory worship practices. Edwards (2009) examined the extent to which two worship practices, verbal affirmation and spontaneous physical worship, are distinctive to African-American congregations and the characteristics associated with these worship practices in contemporary congregations. Both the cultural repertoire and religious marketplace perspectives provide explanations for why religious groups may deploy certain worship elements over others. Where the cultural repertoire perspective emphasizes group connection, the religious marketplace perspective says that the voluntary and competitive nature of American religion encourages religious groups to draw upon certain practices to attract attendees.

The results from Edwards (2009)'s study show that contemporary African-American congregations that practice spontaneous physical worship tend to be larger than other African-American congregations. While spontaneous physical worship is core to the religiocultural repertoires of African Americans, it may also help African-American congregations be more successful in the religious market place. Ethno cultural heritage is less important for verbal affirmation; religious tradition is more important. More than half of all white congregations participate in verbal affirmation, and over 75 percent of white conservative Protestant congregations do so. Only African-American congregations affiliated with African-American-controlled denominations were more likely than white congregations to practice verbal affirmation. Verbal affirmation is an important worship element for white conservative Protestant congregations; practicing verbal affirmation is consistent with what would be expected for a religious tradition rooted in revivalist religion. Chaves' s (2004) ecological model for explaining congregational worship suggests that evidence of more enthusiastic worship expression in congregations corresponds to historical religious developments.

Emerging religious traditions have become steadily enthusiastic over the years in an effort to distinguish themselves from more traditional religions. Congregations within conservative Protestant traditions may be drawing upon more enthusiastic worship to distinguish themselves from congregations in the older, more established religious traditions, namely, Catholicism and liberal Protestant traditions, as they compete in the religious marketplace. Additionally, the factors associated with ecstatic, participatory worship possibly indicate that the meaning and context of ecstatic, participatory worship vary and may have changeover recent decades for some congregations.

Contemporary African-American congregations that participate in ecstatic, participatory worship are the more religiously and socio-politically progressive African-American congregations. They have livelier, energetic services, indicated by their strong emphasis on music and the arts. They are more politically active and more committed to promoting racial and ethnic identification. All of these qualities are facilitated by their younger attendees, higher attendance, and greater wealth. They have large numbers of attendees who can provide the time and youthful energy to invest in and deploy a variety of worship elements that increase the vitality of their worship experience. Comprising nearly 60 percent of all African-American congregations, they represent the mainstream among African-American congregations (Edwards, 2009).

This is a far different picture than that which researchers of African-American worship expected during the early and mid-20th century, or even during more recent decades. Spontaneous physical worship has been associated with smaller (Daniel, 1942; Drake & Cayton, 1970; Nelson, 1996) and less educated African-American congregations (Daniel, 1942; Drake & Cayton, 1970). This study suggests that the meaning of ecstatic, participatory worship among African-American congregations as a marginal, lower-class worship practice may have transformed to reflect innovation, wealth, and social and racial consciousness among contemporary African-American congregations. Given the positive association between spontaneous physical worship and participation in social activities among contemporary African-American congregations, spontaneous physical worship may be the worship element that African- American congregations draw upon to build a sense of connection among congregants.

In some aspects white congregations that participate in ecstatic, participatory worship are similar to African-American congregations that do so. They are younger congregations, invest more in music, and they have greater human resources. Ecstatic, participatory worship in white congregations is clearly associated with the Great Awakening movements of the 18th and 19th centuries (Edwards, 2009, p. 48). Contemporary white congregations that participate in this kind of worship are more likely to be conservative Protestant, located in the South, and believe in the Bible, which have in common with revivalist religion of the time. Their attendees are also less educated. Therefore, traditional explanations for ecstatic, participatory worship are still relevant for understanding the ecstatic, participatory worship practices of contemporary white congregations.

The younger the congregation is, the more likely he or she participates in verbal affirmation and spontaneous physical worship. This is true for African-American and white congregations. For white congregations, the effect of age on ecstatic, participatory worship likely has more to do with the increased desire for an affective religion among younger whites (Beauvoir, 1998). Younger white congregations are adopting more effusive forms of worship as a means of constructing a more emotional worship. By drawing upon these practices, they also distinguish themselves from older white congregations. For African Americans, the difference in age composition is also astonishing.

This form of worship is generally regarded as a traditional form of worship, commonly associated with older African-American congregants. Even though congregations with greater proportions of young adults are more likely to practice ecstatic, participatory worship, older congregants are still the ones participating in this practice in contemporary African-American congregations. As the more mainstream congregations of today, African-American congregations that accommodate ecstatic, anticipatory worship practices are attracting more African Americans of all ages, not just the youth. Although the proportion of older people is less in African-American congregations that participate in ecstatic, participatory worship, the larger congregations still have older attendees. With older attendees, it is likely that someone will participate in this practice during a worship service (Edwards, 2009).

Religion is quite central to ethnicity construction. Certain worship practices among African-American congregations, particularly spontaneous physical worship, are markers of ethnicity rather than religious identity. Among African-American congregations, spontaneous physical worship is a cultural symbol that represents ethnic identity, and defines what it means to be an African-American Christian or even an African American more in general. This resilient part of the religio-cultural repertoires of a majority of African-American congregation seems to signify progressiveness and racial identity. Verbal affirmations are more commonly expressed in African-American congregations than spontaneous physical worship but it is not unique to African-American congregations. It is one of particular religious expressions. We cannot think of spontaneous physical worship and verbal affirmation as having similar historical roots. Congregations access elements from their ethno cultural and religious repertoires to construct their worship experiences and build a sense of community, and to stake a place in the American religious structure (Cornell & Hartmann, 1998; Edwards, 2009).

Ethnicity informs the elements contained in cultural repertoires by establishing group boundaries (Nagel, 1994). In addition to a claim to common ancestry and shared historical past, ethnic groups invoke cultural symbols to foster a sense of community among their members, and to provide a sense of meaning to their ethnicity (Cornell & Hartmann, 1998; Nagel, 1994). Certain cultural symbols are seized as the elements that "epitomize" their sense of peoplehood (Cornell & Hartmann, 1998). Religious practices are often central to this process (Cornell & Hartmann, 1998; Yinger, 1995) and ethnic groups access these practices in their cultural repertoires to construct a sense of "what we are" (Nagel, 1994, p. 162).

Religious marketplace dynamics are also used to explain why congregations practice certain worship elements. This perspective emphasizes that the American religious structure, coming out of the separation of church and state, is voluntary. The voluntary nature of American religion encourages a religious marketplace. People can join the religious group that best meets their needs. This leaves religious groups to compete for potential attendees (Finke & Stark, 1988, 1992; Warner, 1993). Consequently, competition is at the core of American religion. Successful religious groups where success is measured by number of adherents specialize in niches that appeal to individuals from certain demographic groups. This ultimately facilitates "social space for cultural pluralism" (Warner, 1993, p. 202). However, while religion in the United States provides opportunities for cultural diversity, this outcome is more an institutional phenomenon than a cultural one (Warner, 1993).

Each of these perspectives—cultural repertoires, ethnicity, and the religious marketplace—helps us to understand why religious groups deploy certain worship elements over others. They are not necessarily exclusive. Taken together, as suggested by the cultural repertoire and religious marketplace perspectives, African American congregations draw upon unique worship practices to build a sense of community and to stake a place in the American religious structure.

7. Religion and Racial Integration

The unique history of African Americans in the United States has invited much of the discussion on the relationship between religion and race in diverse congregations (Tranby & Hartmann, 2008). The current research on multiracial churches started with Emerson and Smith's (2000) assessment of the potential for black-white integration within American Protestant Christianity. They claimed that the possibility of black-white churches is remote as individualistic orientation toward social change, especially among evangelicals. Emerson (2006) and Edwards (2008b) further argued that achieving true religious integration between blacks and whites seems nearly impossible.

In this regard, we can raise the following questions: "What is the relationship between religion and race for African Americans in this multiracial congregation?; More specifically, "does African-American religious participation in adverse Protestant congregation require reinforcement of racial identity or does religious involvement move them toward transcending the idea of race?"

While religious imperatives can prompt members to participate in racially diffuse congregations, the distinctiveness of the African-American experience in white-dominant American society appears to require multiracial congregations to construct diversity-affirming "havens" such that blacks are affirmed, protected, and even entertained in ways that acknowledge a shared African- American heritage.

Marti (2005) regards the experiences of religious racial integration in Protestant churches as a process by which members of ethno-racial groups subsume their contrasting ethnic identities to a shared religious identity. Ethnicity, not "race" is a complex aspect of the self that can be highlighted or obscured, constructed or reconfigured, guided by interests involving social status and social mobility according to the demands and constraints of presentation (Alexander, 1992; Conzen et al., 1992; Fenton, 1999; Lacy, 2007; Leonard, 1992; McCall & Simmons, 1978; Nagel, 1994, 1996; Royce, 1982; Sollors, 1989; Stryker, 1981).

Individuals connect to congregations by taking opportunities for relational interactions that appeal to at least one aspect of their social selves. Diverse congregations construct relational "havens" which are defined as situation that ally specific arenas of interaction from the interests, beliefs, values, and life circumstances and that ally people together regardless of ancestral heritages. Havens therefore exhibit an interesting dualism as self-selective mechanisms that draw certain people. Over time, member participation in church obscures their ethnic identifications and brings out other valued aspects of their personal identity, and ultimately a shared religious identity becomes more important than their disparate racial identities (see Marti, 2005, 2008b, 2009a). In Marti's arguments, the process of ethnic transcendence depends on havens being racially neutral.

In contrast to Marti's approach to ethno racial identity, both Emerson (2006) and Edwards (2008b) proposed racial formation and critical race theories to highlight how "race" is more significant than "ethnicity." Edwards sparsely defines 'race' as oriented around "claims of shared culture, history, or common descent "to understand American society and to demonstrate how the structural advantages of being white extend to the structure of black white churches (Bonilla-Silva, 2003; Doane, 1997; Lewis, 2004; Lipsitz, 1998; Omi & Winant, 1994).

Edwards (2008b) claims that "race" should be a central and determining structural characteristic if we have a clear and proper understanding of "whiteness" and the racial hierarchies and boundaries that resulted throughout U.S.. Edwards further argues that African Americans must adopt white-dominant cultural norms and practices in order to fit into this integrated church, and insists that race is not viewed as a particular characteristic of African Americans but rather as a dominating one.

Being black in America is not simply one aspect of identity but rather overwhelms the identity of a person that religion largely fails to address. Everett Hughes (1945) classically formed the concept of "master status" focusing on how racial stigma overwhelms other markers of prestige through observations of how whites treated African Americans in professional occupations. (Du Bois, 2003; Fanon, 1965, 1967). What W. E. B. DuBois (2003, p. 204) called "the problem of the color line" remains evident in studies on the pervasive social consequences of segregation and stigmatization based on skin color, legal definitions of whiteness, and institutionalized racism (see Lewis, 1995; Bobo, Kluegel, & Smith, 1997; Drake & Cayton, 1945; Freeman et al., 1966; Hunter, Allen, & Telles, 2001; Keith & Herring, 1991; Lopez, 1996)

African Americans who attempt to assimilate into a white culture must make a cultural leap and still experience prejudice and discrimination (Feagin & Sikes, 1995). Because African Americans are "involuntary minorities" who are painfully aware of their disadvantaged status in comparison to native majority whites (Kao & Tienda, 1998; Massey et al., 2003; Ogbu, 1978, 1981), African Americans experience and alienation that cannot be compared to other racial/ethnic groups (Yancey, 2003a). Emerson (2006) and Edwards (2008b) claim that religious communities need to accentuate the distinctive racial experiences of African Americans and create hospitable environments that explicitly welcome and incorporate them (see also DeYoung et al., 2003; Yancey, 2003b). Both stress that non-whites joining diverse congregations are not "race traitors" who wish to deny their ethno racial distinctive but these members want to affirm the "uniqueness" of their racial identity "while at the same time being around people from other cultures" at church (Emerson, 2006, p. 129).

Emerson (2006, pp. 168-169) provides a list of ethnic reinforcement mechanisms founding multiracial churches (see also Yancey 2003b). Emerson primarily argues that interracial churches must make a clearly stated institutional commitment to racial equity and create structures to ensure that equity. Emerson issues a two-fold call: whites should accede privileges for the sake of marginalized nonwhite groups, and blacks as well as other oppressed minorities should avoid victimization and take bold initiatives to create racially affirming, integrated religious communities. Furthermore, congregational leaders are said to be central to cultivating integrated congregations by personally committing to racial equity, creating forums where racial issues are actively discussed, and actively managing member commitment toward common religious goals.

Edwards (2008b, p. 137) similarly urges interracial church leaders to "select African Americans as key contributors to the process" of creating an environment of racial inclusion to counter white hegemony. In resisting "white normative and structural dominance," she calls interracial churches "where the culture and experiences of all racial groups are not just tolerated, but appreciated." Tranby and Hartmann (2008) also apply whiteness studies and critical race theory to the possibility of black-white congregations, specifically arguing that racial identity should be highlighted and affirmed rather than merely subsumed under the auspices of religion.

Given the contradictory assertions between these two perspectives, the question remains: does religious racial integration require transcending racial specificity in favor of religious unity?; Or is there perhaps a more dynamic relationship between the processes of ethnic transcendence and ethnic reinforcement that remains to be uncovered?

Race does not disappear as being important for these church members, but it does not become a master status for those who join diverse congregations (Marti, 2009b). The distinctiveness of the African-American experience in white-dominant American society appears to require multiracial congregations to construct relational havens in such a way that blacks are affirmed, protected, and perhaps even entertained. Rather than conceptually allowing only for racially neutral havens it is important to expand on Marti's notion of havens to allow for racially affirming havens (see Marti 2009b, pp. xii-xv). Thus, the congregation does not merely practice ethnic reinforcement but also the congregation places the value of diversity at the center of the congregation in a way that recognizes the unique experience of African Americans. Recently, research has shown African-American worship practices like spontaneous physical worship are ethnically distinct (Edwards, 2009). Historically, much of the Black Church's ministry involved political mobilization and corporate empowerment since the oppression of blacks in American society is what prompted the development of the Black Church (Harris, 1999; Patillo-McCoy, 1998).

Although we should not assume these churches are homogeneous, scholars of African-American religious history have long argued that these churches have a shared tradition within Christianity and are fundamental to the collective experience of African Americans in the United States (Lincoln & Mamiya, 1990, p. 45; Pinn, 2002, p. xii). The experience of racism led to a collective solidarity and obligation to support one another. Moreover, research supports that black identity is stronger for African Americans involved in traditional black denominations (Ellison, 1991). For this reason, distinctions within the African-American experience cannot be ignored.

In short, in multiracial churches that promote the value of diversity, ethnic reinforcement functions to attract race-conscious participants who eventually move toward processes of ethnic transcendence and congregational integration. This presents a more comprehensive understanding of both processes of transcendence and reinforcement. The issue of "race" is openly acknowledged in the church and the races should come together through corporate initiatives that emphasize the religious, nonracial aspects of their identity. We may anticipate that congregations that successfully integrate African Americans have racially affirming havens centered on the value of diversity. However, in order for these congregations to become and remain multiracial, they must deploy their religious resources to enable members to adopt nonracially based identities as well (Ganiel, 2010). Accommodating for the racial distinctiveness of African Americans through such havens affirms Edwards's (2008b, p. 99) finding that "people of different races can worship together, even when the salience of racial identity drastically differs across racial groups."

Christerson et al. (2005) also conclude that analytically sepparating ethnically transcendent from ethnically reinforcing dynamics accentuates that racially specific identity can be affirmed in a racially diverse setting and may even be necessary for sustaining cross-ethnic relationships. The numerical minorities in the multiracial congregations they studied were more likely to remain if they had safe social spaces within the congregation to connect with people of their same race/ethnicity. This suggests that ethnic reinforcement is important for any ethnic group that is in the numerical minority such as African Americans.

Members of all ethno racial groups may love the music, but African-American members resonate with the music as connected with their racial identity as worshippers in the Black Church. The complexity of multiracial congregations, therefore, includes the manner in which racial specificity is negotiated within the constraints of calling forth broadly shared religious connections that attempt to be racially neutral. Researchers have long argued that certain ethno racial groups like African Americans constitute distinct cultural groups in America to develop their own heritages in the context of a Eurocentric American society (Hunter et al., 2001; Porter & Washington, 1993; Sanders, 2002; Takaki, 1979; Tuan, 1998; Vigil, 1998).

Black-white congregations cannot escape the power dynamics still operative in the larger society. Perhaps truly integrated black-white churches are not possible in the United States. It is not possible that these churches equally acknowledge, equally assert, and equally value the distinctive ethno racial backgrounds and experiences of each group.

It appears that the never-ending issue of race for many African Americans makes pluralism including separate and distinct elements of all racial cultures present a more likely outcome for black-white Protestant congregations than integration maintains aspects of separate cultures while creating a new culture (DeYoung et al., 2003, pp. 164-69).

While DeYoung et al.(2003) offer alternative models of a multiethnic church, it may be more appropriate to say that too strictly isolating the dynamics embedded within these ideal-type models can not account for the intersecting and interwoven dynamics that occur in diverse congregations. This study has highlighted the interplay between religious and racial identity in the experience of African Americans at Oasis, but there are other factors that may shed light on the dynamics observed in this congregation.

Demographic characteristics of age, class neighborhood, and percentage of mixed marriages are examples of important variables that may affect the integration of African Americans into multiracial churches, but external social factors alone are not sufficient to accomplish diversity (Dougherty & Huyser, 2008). Therefore, there needs to employ a more varied conceptual lens, to discover subtle, racially specific arenas of interaction and recognition being continually reaffirmed among members in diverse congregations that would otherwise remain hidden to observers, particularly when they are not members of that ethno-racial group.

8. African American Church and Community Activism

This section will discuss the African American Church's relevance in the contemporary black community, more specifically the role of religiosity in encouraging community activism among contemporary African Americans. The African American church provided a venue for blacks to express themselves politically and permitted community engagement through a variety of the church's organizations. Based on the auxiliary organizations, the African American Church encouraged community activism on a limited basis among its members. In this respect, it can be expected that the Black Church will continue to promote and encourage communal activism as part of its cultural heritage (Swain, 2008).

The community activism in the African American community preceded political activism, and it was facilitated after civil rights legislation removed legal barriers to political participation in 1965. In the present, the Black Church has been the catalyst for encouraging community activism among African Americans. Black churches play a significant role in encouraging social and community activism: Churches provide an important incubator for civic skills, civic, norms, community interests and civic recruitment religiously; active men and women learn to give speeches, run meetings, manage disagreements, and bear administrative responsibility. In this regards, churchgoers are substantially more likely to be involved in secular organizations, to vote and participate politically in other ways, and to have deeper informal social connections (Putnam, 2000, p 67).

Churches, more than any other American institution, are able to facilitate membership in secular organizations. For example, churches transmit messages that support civic norms that stress the importance of community activism. They also instill civic skills that are transferable to secular institutions, and the social networks in churches facilitate recruitment into other forms of community and social involvement (Putnam, 2000). The Black Church was indispensable in rallying the black community in the struggle for civil rights in the late 1950s and early 1960s. Black churches, led by social conscious ministers, were responsible for the increase in membership in civil rights organizations such as SNCC and the NAACP (Morris, 1984).

Black Church was especially important to the black community because it provided the backdrop for many social and community activities. In these cases, secular organizations such as the NAACP and the SCLC (Southern Christian Leadership Conference) met in church halls and basements (Lincoln & Mamiya, 1990). Thus, the black church has been the center of social, economic, and community activity of black Americans.

However, there were views of the African American Church as an opiate, discouraging social and political activism among adherents. The Black Church is an institution that sought to strike a conciliatory tone with the racist institutions in order to ensure its survival (Woodson, 1945). Even though the church was palace of refuge from the deluge of insults and indignities blacks constantly endured, it sought to instill parishioners with other-worldly orientation that did much to edify parishioners spiritually but virtually nothing to encourage social and community activism (Frazier, 1963).

There were other claims that religion, religious institutions, and religious leaders encourage avoidance and escapism, that is, otherworldliness rather than activism. (Frazier, 1962; Marx,

1967; Myrdal, 1944). The churches generally provide individuals with emotional reprieve from the pain of injustice, while at the same time supporting the maintenance of the status quo and lessening efforts to subvert unjust social arrangements (Marx, 1990). In addition, church attendance depresses community activism, which suggests that religious affiliation, in and of itself, is unlikely to facilitate community activism (Harris, 1999).

Before the 1960s and the success of the Civil Rights Movement, blacks found refuge, solace and courage to resist oppression and racism through the influence of the Black Church's prophetic voice (Swain, 2008). The fact that the church was often monitored by racist law enforcement officials meant that the church was often forced to employ varying degrees of subtlety in raising that voice. Nevertheless, the Black Church was often the leading voice in advocating the course of action that might best rectify conditions of racial injustice confronting blacks at any given time. Where churches were at the vanguard of resisting racial discrimination and oppression, they were led by pastors who advocated social and community involvement. These clergy preached a social gospel that encouraged joining and participating in civil rights organizations such as the NAACP. They encouraged the formation of auxiliary organizations as a viable way to address problems in the black community. In many cases, black clergymen often served as organizers and leaders of local

NAACP chapters (Morris, 1984; Lincoln & Mamiya, 1990; Mamiya, 1999; Swain, 2008).

In this regard, we can see how important the church was in providing the personnel support necessary to sustain strong secular organizations. Moreover, as one of the primary agents of socialization in the black community, we might expect African American churches to be positively associated with membership in secular organizations such as the NAACP. The exclusion of blacks from the social, economic, and political mainstream of society in the first half of the twentieth century would have fostered the sense of shared status. The appeals for membership in organizations whose emphasis was on resisting the policies that contributed to racial inequality were not likely to go unheeded. This in part provides a framework for understanding how members in politicized black churches would respond to appeals by clergy to join organizations such as the NAACP (Wald, 2003). Participation in the church's auxiliary groups provided the skills and interpersonal skills, and sense of shared experience that would have facilitated memberships in civil rights and other local grass roots organizations. Thus, the historical proximity of the church to community organizations suggests that the Black Church will be positively associated with community activism and that politicized churches will show a stronger connection with community activism than non-politicized black churches (Swain, 2008).

Since a component of the prophetic message is derived from the pulpits of these churches, the members take the responsibility to join organizations to seek the improvement of the black community such as the NAACP. For instance, Dr. Martin L. King, encouraged a politicized atmosphere at Dexter Avenue Baptist in Montgomery, AL and Ebenezer Baptist in Atlanta, GA. Taylor Branch (1989) points out that one of the very first things King did upon assuming the pastorate at Dexter Avenue Baptist was to create a committee that acted as liaison with the local NAACP branch. Dr. Martin L. King announced that all members should register to vote. The latter initiative is remarkable given the time in which it occurred in 1955 when such an exhortation was viewed as illegal by the wider white community and could have been personally dangerous for King.

African American religiosity has had relevancy in the post Civil-Rights era. As desegregation policies and affirmative action policies were implemented in the 1970s, African Americans' standard of living improved, sparking urban sprawl and the dispersion of the black community throughout the USA. One of the results of the dispersion and fragmentation of the black community was a deterioration of the relevancy of the Black Church in the everyday lives of Black Americans. Indeed, research has born out that religiosity among Black Americans has declined since the 1970s (Putnam, 2000).

However, patterns of religiosity among the children of baby boomers in the African American community simply mirrors that of their generational cohort in the broader society in that they are less religiously inclined than their parents (Putnam, 2000). Therefore, declining religiosity has not only affected the black community, but the wider American society as a whole. While religiosity may have experienced a decline in the black community, when it comes to facilitating community activism, the Black Church remains an institutional force to be reckoned with in the African American community.

There may be a distinction between politicized and non-politicized black churches in that politicized black churches seem to have a stronger impact on community activism. Since the end of the civil rights era, scholars have debated whether or not the Black Church has been conducive to the quest of the black community for civil and material based rights. The prophetic Black Church of the civil rights era was led by socially activist minded clergy such as King, Jesse Jackson, and Al Sharpton.

On the contrary, there were clergies such as T. D. Jakes and Creflo Dollar who seem to have rejected the former's social activism and replaced it into a materialistic, prosperity based gospel that seems interested only in increasing the individual prosperity. The ministry of black contemporary clergy such as Jakes and Dollar does not appear to be as concerned with social problems affecting the black community stemming from racial prejudice and inequality. Therefore, they may not be as likely to encourage their parishioners to become socially and politically active through organizations such as the NAACP.

By viewing the Black Church as a multi-dimensional religious institution, we can accommodate the perspectives of both views. The Black Church is comprised of both politicized churches that are more likely to encourage and facilitate social activism and non-politicized churches that have other-worldly emphases and orientations. Thus, viewing the Black Church as a multi-dimensional institution, having different and in some cases divergent agendas, both camps are correct in their argument.

Then, has the Black Church lost its prophetic voice? The Black Church's prophetic role is no less diminished today than it was during the late 1950s when it was at the vanguard of the black community's struggle for civil rights. It appears that black churches, and especially politicized black churches continue to promote social and community activism by encouraging parishioners to join civil rights organizations and other community based organizations in the black community. One of the most pressing challenges facing the Black Church today is maintaining its relevance in a black community that is increasingly divided by socio-economic status (Lincoln & Mamiya, 1990). If a link can be found between social status and church selection, it may or may not facilitate our understanding of the multi-dimensional nature of religiosity among Black Americans (Swain, 2008, p. 410).

Ever since the politicized church provided support to slaves on ante-bellum plantations and to downtrodden blacks in de facto segregated USA long after the abolition of slavery, African American religious institutions have provided an outlet for social and political expression for the African American community. The Black church seems to have stood the test of time as it sustains its viability in the African American community in the last decade of the 1990s and the first decade of a new millennium. There is no reason to doubt that this trend by the African American church of being a primary facilitator of community and social activism will continue in the foreseeable future (Swain, 2008).

07

Conclusion

Though Africans and their descendants lived and labored in the mainland colonies and later the new nation from the seventeenth century, large-scale conversions of African American people occurred during the eighteenth and nineteenth centuries. Prior to that time, most Blacks were not Christian. Under the impulse of revivalism with strong emphasis on inward conversion, a great number of blacks accepted Christianity during the eighteenth and nineteenth centuries. The religious revivals were based on the belief: God would save all who believed in Him and the souls of all men are equal before God. By heavily stressing the inward conversion experience the revival tended to deemphasize the outward status of men which caused black and white alike to feel personally that Christ had died for them as individuals.

Emphasizing the conversion experience instead of the process of religious instruction also allowed illiterate slaves more access to Christianity. The evangelicalism preached by revivalists appealed a lot to black slaves.

The Christianity accepted by blacks was not the white version with slavery but their own religion which was made out of the harsh reality under the slave system and their African tradition. In the face of day to day drudgery and occasional brutality, blacks were sure that God never forgave slavery and would end it. Blacks firmly believed in God who would save and liberate them from bondage.

The inward conversion of revival confirmed the slave' value as a human and his worth as one of the chosen of God. African-American identity was based on the biblical story of Israel's enslavement and Exodus from Egypt. Black Americans were symbolized as Israelites in Egypt destined for some special task under the protection of God. The images of the chosen people offered an insight into the kind of weapons the slaves had to prevent themselves from internalizing the stereotyped images which their master foisted upon.

The black Christianity was not confined to any specific time or place, but was appropriate to almost every situation. This notion of transcendence reached the essence of slave religion. Unable to take an adjustment to the external world involving meaningful forms of personal integration, attainment of status and feelings of individual worth, the slaves created a new world by transcending their narrow confines where they were forced to live, and protected their personalities from some of the worst ravages of the slave system.

Black Christianity was much more than asylums from the spirit of slavery. The black evangelicals tried to find freedom of thought, freedom of speech, freedom of action, and freedom for the development of a true "Christian manhood" connected with the exercise of political rights. Black evangelicals in the North organized under three issues: Antislavery, anti-colonization, and moral reform. On the other hand, in the South, the situation of the slaves was appropriately depicted in Moses' words to the Israelites of the Red Sea: "Stand still and see the salvation of God." (Raboteau, 1980, 1987, 2000)

Christianity fostered acquiescence as well as acts of resistance both in the same slave. Suppression may easily force outward acquiescence but internal rebellion is virtually impossible to control. The inner world of slaves was the fundamental battleground and there evangelicalism functioned as an important weapon in defending psychological, emotional and moral freedom of the slaves in the brutal system.

The essence of black evangelicalism was not ethics but liturgy. Ecstatic behavior in the form of spirit possession was central to the liturgy of slave evangelicals. The African heritage of dance was expressed in the evangelical religion of the American slaves in the ring shout and similar patterns of ecstatic behavior. The dance of shout played a significant role of connecting the core of African religion-spirit possession to the core of evangelicalism-conversion experience. In the spirituals also, African style and European hymns met and became a new African-American song. Even as the gods of Africa gave way to the God of Christianity, the African heritage of singing, dancing, spirit possession continued to influence Afro-American spirituals, ring shouts, and folk beliefs.

This proved the slaves' ability not only to adapt to new contexts but to do so creatively. Also it proved that blacks had an active role in creating their culture in America. The strategies to survive under slavery and racial oppression combined with their African heritage gave birth to African-American Christianity distinguished from white's, which established an identity and meaning for Afro-Americans and a challenge to American racism.

Spirituality has played an important role in connecting African American people. Along with commitment, love, and affection, spirituality is also believed to reduce the perceived stressful situations of caring and is an important reason for African American family members' provision of care. (Peirce, 2001). Spirituality is composed of formal Christian beliefs and the secular value of care for one's own. The spirituals are transforming and transformational (Archbold, 1995). In the spirituals, as well as in the sermons of Black preachers and in the chanted prayers of congregations, the words, stories and language of American Christianity were bonded with African artistic and ritual forms. The rhythms and tones of the preachers' voices and of the congregations' singing, the danced movements and the handclaps and tapped beats were all African, even though the message was seemingly Christian. The experience of possession or intimacy with spirit is still the hallmark of African American Christianity.

For African Americans, both during slavery and in its long aftermath, church has functioned as a supporter of a social and political mobilizations as well as spiritual and community orientation. African Americans have found themselves in conflict over interpretation of symbols and norms, public behavior, coping strategies, and a variety of political acts of resistance to structures of domination. The black churches provide a home for thousands of people transplanted by the circumstances of their upward mobility in their economic pursuits. These churches offer a place where their personal, familial and spiritual needs are met where their children can experience a rich environment for their spiritual and moral development. Further, these churches provide an ideal place for politicians and others to rally and have the wherewithal to make change not only on the individual but also on the larger societal level. African American churches still serve as a beacon of hope and community empowerment.

Thus, African American religion has been the means by which one remembers and cultivates an alternative understanding of one's humanity confronting constant disdains and denials. African American religion is not limited to the institutional church, but spread across the breadth of culture, family, community, and language. This meaning of religion nourishes another experience of reality that nurtures connection to the divine and constitutes a truly human identity.

Bibliography

Alexander, Claire E. 1992. *The art of "being black": The creation of black British youth identities.* Oxford, NY: Oxford University Press.

Alexander, Shawn. 2008. *The Afro-American Agitator: A Collection of Writings, 1880-1928.* In: T. Thomas Fortune (Ed.). Gainesville: University Press of Florida,

Anderson, Elijah. 1997. *Streetwise: Race, Class, and Change in an Urban Community.* The University of Chicago Press.

Anderson, Robert M. 1979. *Vision of the disinherited: The making of American Pentecostalism.* New York: Oxford University Press.

Angell, Stephen W. 1992. *Bishop Henry McNeal Turner and African-American Religion in the South.* Knox-ville: University of Tennessee Press.

Auerbach, Erich. 1953. *Mimesis: The Representation of Reality in Western Literature.* Princeton: Princeton University Press.

Baer, Hans A., & Merrill Singer. 1992. *African American Religion in the Twentieth Century: Varieties of Protest and Accommodation.* Knox-ville: Univesiry of Tennessee Press.

Baird, Robert & Alfred Bloom. 1971. *Indian and Far Eastern Religious Traditions.* New York: Harper & Row.

Baird, Robert D. 1971. *Category Formation in the History of Religions.* The Hague: Mouton.

Bakhtin, Mikhail. 1994. *The Bakhtin Reader. Pam Morris* (Ed.). London: Edward Arnold.

Baldwin, Lewis. 1984. 'A Home in Dat Rock': Afro-American Folk Sources and Slave Visions of Heaven and Hell. *Journal of Religious Thought* 41(1), 38-57.

Ball, J., L. Armistead, & Austin, B. 2003. The Relationship Between Religiosity and Adjustment Among African- American, Female, Urban Adolescents. *Journal of Adolescence* 26, 431-46.

Barrett, Justin L. 1999. Theological correctness: Cognitive constraint and the study of religion. *Method & Theory in the Study of Religion* 11, 325-339.

Barthes, Roland. 1973. *Elements of Semiology*. Annette Lavers & Colin Smith (Trans.). New York: Hill & Wang.

Batson, C. Daniel, Schoenrade, Patricia & Ventis, W. Larry. 1993. *Religion and the Individual: A Social-Psychological Perspective.* Oxford: Oxford University Press.

Beaudoin, John. 1998. Evil, the Human Cognitive Condition, and Natural Theology. *Religious Studies* 34(4), 403-418.

Bennet, Robert A. 1995. Black Experience and the Bible. In: Gayraud Wilmore (Ed.), *African American Religious Studies: An Interdisciplinary Anthology,* Duke University Press. pp. 129-139.

Berger, P. L. 1967 *The Social Reality of Religion*. London: Farber and Farber.

Billingsley, Andrew. 1992. *Climbing Jacob's Ladder: The Enduring Legacy of African-American Families*. New York: Touchstone Book.

________. 1999. *Mighty Like a River: The Black Church and Social Reform.* Oxford: Oxford University Press.

Birchett, Colleen. 1992. *Biblical strategies for a community in crisis:*

What African Americans can do? Chicago: Urban Ministries Inc.

Blaine, B., & Crocker. J. 1995. Religiousness, Race, and Psychological Well-Being: Exploring Social Psychological Mediators. *Personality and Social Psychology Bulletin* 21(10), 1031-1041.

Blight, David W. 2001. *Race and Reunion: The Civil War in American Memory.* Cambridge, MA: The Belknap Press of Harvard University Press.

Blum, Edward J. 2005. 'O God of a Godless Land': Northern African American Challenges to White Christian Nationhood, 1865-1906. In: Edward J. Blum and W.Scott. Poole. (Eds.) *Vale of Tears: New Essays on Religion and Reconstruction*, Macon: Mercer Univesity Press.

Bobo, L., Kluegel, J. R. & Smith, R. A. 1997. Laissez-Faire racism: The crystallization of a kinder, gentler anti-black ideology. In: S. A. Tuch & J. K. Martin. (Eds.), *Racial attitudes in the 1990s.* Westport CO, Praeger, pp.16-42.

Boles, John B. 1972. *The Great Revival, 1787-1805: The Origins of the Southern Evangelical Mind.* Lexington: University Press of Kentucky.

Bonilla-Silva, Eduardo. 2003. *Raicsm Without Racists*. Lanham, MD: Rowman & Littlefield.

Boyatzis, C. J. 2006 Advancing Our Understanding of Religious Dynamics in the Family and Parent-Child Relationship. *The International Journal for the Psychology of Religion* 16(4), pp. 245-251.

Boyd, Robert. 1998. The Storefront Church Ministry in African American Communities of the Urban North During the Great Migration: The Making of an Ethnic Niche. *The Social Science*

Journal 35(3), 319-332.

Boyd-Franklin, N., & Lockwood, T. 1999. Spirituality and religion: Implications for psychotherapy with African American clients and families. In: F. Walsh (Ed.), *Spiritual resources in family therapy.* New York: Guilford.

Boyer, Pascal. 2001. *Religion Explained: The Evolutionary Origins of Religious Thought.* New York: Basic Books.

Brandt, Per Aage & Brandt, Line. 2002. *Making Sense of a Blend in Apparatur: Tidsskrift for litteratur og kulturr 4(2).* Odense: Denmark.

Brent, Joseph. 1993. *Charles Sanders Peirce: A Life*, Bloomington: Indiana University Press.

Bridges, L. J., & Moore, K. A. 2002. *Religion and spirituality in childhood and adolescence*. Washington, DC: Child Trends.

Brodsky, A. E. 2000 *T*he Role of Religion in the Lives of Resilient, Urban, African American, Single Mothers. *Journal of Community Psychology* 28(2), 199-219.

Brodsky, A. E., & DeVet, K. S. 2000 You Have to be Real Strong: Parenting Goals and Strategies of Resilient, Urban, African American, Single Mothers. *Journal of Prevention and Intervention in the Community* 20(1-2), 159-178.

Brooks, Walter H. The Evolution of the Negro Baptist Church. *The Journal of Negro History* 7(1), 11-22.

Buchler, Justus. 1955. *Nature and Judgment,* New York: Columbia University Press.

________. 1969. On a Strain of Arbitrariness in Whitehead's System. *Southern Journal of Philosophy,* 66(19), 589-601.

Buller, Cornelius A. 1996. *The Unit of Nature and History in Pannenberg's Theology*, Lanham, MD: Littlefield Adams Books.

Burger, W. R., & Youkeles, M. 2000. *Human Services in Contemporary America.* Pacific Grove, CA: Brooks/Cole.

Butler, Jonathan. 1990. *Awash in a Sea of Faith: Christianizing the American People.* Cambridge, Massachusetts: Harvard University Press.

Butler, Jonathan. 1991. *Softly and Tenderly Jesus is Calling: Heaven and Hell in American Revivalism, 1870-1920.* Brooklyn: Carlson Pub.

Cade, J. B. 1935. Out of the mouths of the ex-slaves. *Journal of Negroes History* 20, 394-337.

Calhoun-Brown, Allison. 1998. While Marching to Zion: Otherworldliness and Racial Empowerment in the Black Community. *Journal for the Scientific Study of Religion* 37(3), 427-39.

________. 1999. The Image of God: Black Theology and Racial Empowerment in the African American Community. *Review of Religious Research* 40(3), 97-211.

Carlson, T. D., D. Kirkpatrick, L. Hecker, L., & Killmer, M. 2002. Religion, Spirituality, and Marriage and Family Therapy: A Study of Family Therapists' Beliefs about the Appropriateness of Addressing Religious and Spiritual Issues in Therapy. *The American Journal of Family Therapy* 30, 157-171.

Carter, Harold A.1976. *The Prayer Tradition of Black People.* New York: Judison Press.

Cavendish, James. 2000. Church-Based Community Activism: A Comparison of Black and White Catholic Congregations. *Journal for the Scientific Study of Religion* 39(1), 64-77.

Chalfant, H. P., & Hellner, P. L. 1990. The Clergy as a Resource for Those Encountering psychological Distress. *Review of*

Religious Research 31(3), 305-313.

Chatters, L. M., & Taylor, R. J. 2005 *Religion and Families.* In: V. Bengtson, Acock, A., Allen, K., Dillworth-Anderson, P. & Klein, D. (Eds.), *Sourcebook of Family Theory and Research.* Thousand Oaks, Sage, pp. 517-522.

Chatters, L., Levin, J., & Taylor, R. 1992. Antecedents and dimensions of religious involvement among older black adults. *Journal of Gerontology* 47, 269-278.

Chaves, Mark 2004, *Congregation in America*, Boston: Harvard University Press.

Chaves, Mark, & Higgins, Lynn M. 1992. Comparing the Community Involvement of Black and White Congregations. *Journal for the Scientific Study of Religion* 31(4), 425-440.

Chaves, Mark, Mary E. Konieczny, Kraig Beyerlein and Emily Barman. 1999. The National Congregations Study: Background, Methods, and Selected Results. *Journal for the Scientific Study of Religion* 38(4), 458-476.

Chestnutt, Charles. 2008. *The Conjuring Woman.* London: Book Jungle.

Chireau, Yvonne P. 2006. *Black Magic Religion and the African American Conjuring Tradition.* Los Angeles: University of California Press.

Christerson, B, Edwards, KL, & Emerson, MO. 2005. *Against All Odds: The Struggle for Radical Integration in Religious Organizations.* New York: New York University Press

Christerson, Brad & Emerson, Michael O. 2003. The costs of diversity in religious organizations: An in-depth case study. *Sociology of Religion* 64(2), 163-81.

Clemmons, P. 1991. Feminists, spirituality, and the twelve steps of

Alcoholics Anonymous. *Women & Therapy* 11, 97-109.

Clifford, James. 1986. On ethnographic allegory. In: James Clifford & George Marcus (Eds.), *Writing Culture: The Poetics and Politics of Ethnography*. Berkeley, University of California Press, pp. 1-26.

Coalter, M. J. 1995. *How Shall We Witness? Faithful Evangelism in a Reformed Tradition*. Westminster: John Knox.

Cone, James H. 1992. *The Spirituals and the Blues*. Maryknoll: Orbis Books.

________. 1995. Black Theology as Liberation Theology. In: Gayraud Wilmore (Ed.), *African American Religious Studies: An Interdisciplinary Anthology,* Duke University Press, pp. 177-207.

Cone, James. 1970. *A Black Theology of Liberation*. Philadelphia: Lippincott.

Conzen, Kathleen N., David A. Gerber, EwaMorawska, Pozzetta, George E. & Vecolli, Rudolph J. 1992. The invention of ethnicity: A perspective from the USA. *Journal of American Ethnic History* 12(1), 3-41.

Cornell, Stephen and Douglas Hartman. 1998. Mapping the terrain: Definitions. In: Stephen Cornell & Douglas Hartman (Eds.), *Ethnicity and race: Making identities in a changing world,* Thousand Oaks, Pine Forge Press, pp. 15-38.

Corrington, Robert S. 1987a. *The Community of Interpreters: On the Hermeneutics of Nature and the Bible in the American Philosophical Tradition*, Macon, GA: Mercer University Press.

________. 1988. *Semiosis and the Phenomenon of Worldhood, Semiotics.* Lanham, MD: University Press of America.

________.1989. *Faith and the Signs of Expectation, in Semiotics.* Lanham, MD: University Press of America.

________. 1990b. *Transcendence and the Loss of the Semiotic Self*, in *Semiotics*. Lanham, MD: University Press of America.

________. 1992b. *Nature and Spirit: An Essay in Ecstatic Naturalism*, New York: Fordham University Press.

________. 1993a. *An Introduction to C. S. Peirce: Philosopher, Semiotician, and Ecstatic Naturalist*, Lanham, MD: Rowman & Littlefield.

________. 1993b. Beyond Experience: Pragmatism and Nature's God. *American Journal of Theology and Philosophy* 14(2), 147-160.

________. 1994. *Ecstatic Naturalism: Signs of the World, Advances in Semiotics*. Bloomington: Indiana University Press.

________. 1995. Peirce's Ecstatic Naturalism: The Birth of the Divine in Nature. *American Journal of Theology and Religion*, 16(2), 173-187.

Costen, Melva Wilson. 1993. *African American Christian Worship*. Abingdon Press.

________. 1995. Singing Praise to God in African American Worship Contexts. In: Gayraud Wilmore (Ed.), *African American Religious Studies: An Interdisciplinary Anthology*, Duke University Press, pp. 392-404.

Counihan, C. & Van Esterik, P. 1997. *Food and culture: A reader*. New York: Routledge.

Dalton, Sharron. 2006. Eating fast food causes obesity. In: Laura K. Egendorf (Ed.) *Food: opposing viewpoints,* Farmington Hills, MI, Greenhaven Press.

Damasio, Antonio R. 1994. *Descartes' Error: Emotion, Reason, and the Human Brain*. New York: G. P. Putnam.

Danesi, Marcel. 1993. *Messages and Meanings: An Introduction to*

Semiotics. Toronto: Canadian Scholar's Press.

Daniel, Vattel E. 1942. Ritual and stratification in Chicago Negro churches. *American Sociological Review* 7(3), 352-61.

D'Aquili, Euguene & Newberg, Andrew B. 1999. *The Mystical Mind: Probing the Biology of Religious Experience. Theology and the Sciences*. Minneapolis: Fortress Press.

Davies, Paul. 1992. *The Mind of God: The Scientific Basis for a Rational World.* New York: Simon & Schuster.

Day, Katie. 2001. The Construction of Political Strategies Among African American Clergy. In: Sue S. Crawford & Laura R. Olson, *Christian Clergy in American Politics.* Johns Hopkins University Press, pp. 85-103.

Dayton, Donald. 1987. *Theological roots of Pentecostalism.* Grand Rapids, MI: Zondervan.

Dean, William. 1986. *American Religious Empiricism*, Albany: SUNY Press.

________. 1988. *History Making History: The New Historicism in American Religious Thought*, Albany: SUNY Press.

Deely, John. 1990. *Basics of Semiotics*, Bloomington: Indiana University Press.

________. 1994. *The Human Use of Signs: Or Elements of Anthroposemiosis.* Lanham, MD: Rowman & Littlefield.

Delaney, C. F. 1993. *Science, Knowledge, and Mind: A Study in the Philosophy of C. S. Peirce.* NotreDame: University of Notre Dame Press.

Derrida, Jacques. 1967. *De la grammatologie*, Paris: Editions de Minuit.

________. 1982a. *Signature event context. In Margins of Philosophy.*

Chicago: University of Chicago Press.

________. 1982b. *Différance. In Margins of Philosophy*. Chicago: University of Chicago Press.

DeYoung, Curtiss Paul, Michael O. Emerson, George Yancey, & Karen Chai. 2003. *United by faith: Multicultural congregations as a response to the problem of race*. New York: Oxford University Press.

Doane Jr., Ashley W. 1997. Dominant group identity in the United States: The role of hidden ethnicity in intergroup, *The Sociological Quarterly* 38(3), 375-397.

Dollahite, D. C., L. D. Marks, & M. Goodman. 2004. Religiosity and Families: Relational and Spiritual Linkages in a Diverse and Dynamic Cultural Context. In: M. J. Coleman and L. H. Ganong (Eds.), *The Handbook of Contemporary Families*. Thousand Oaks, Sage, pp. 411-431.

Donals, L. & Gelpi, S. J. 1993. Review of my Nature and Spirit: An Essay in Ecstatic Naturalism. *Theological Studies*, 54(2), 369-370.

________. 1997. *Extraordinary Minds*. New York: Basic Books.

Dougherty, Kevin D. & Kimberly R. Huyser. 2008. Racially Diverse Congregations: Organizational Identity and the Accommodation of Differences. *Journal for the Scientific Study of Religion* 47, 23-43.

Drake, St. Clair, & Horace R. Cayton. 1940. *Churches and Voluntary Associations in the Chicago Negro Community*. District 3, Chicago: University of Chicago Press

________. 1942[1962]. *Black Metropolis: A Study of Negro Life in a Northern City* Vol. I & II. New York: Harper & Row.

________. 1970. *Black metropolis: A study of Negro life in a*

northern city. New York: Harcourt, Brace and Company.

Driskill, Todd A. 1994. Beyond the Text: Ecstatic Naturalism and American Pragmatism, *American Journal of Theology and Philosophy*, 15(3), 305-323.

DuBois, W. E. B. 1903[2003]. *The Negro Church*. Walnut Creek: AltaMira Press.

________. 1903. *Souls of Black Folk*. Chicago: McClurg

________. 1994. *Of the Faith of the Fathers. In The Souls of Black Folk*. Chicago: A. C. McClurg & Co.

________. 2001. The Negro Church. *Report of a Social Study Made under the Direction of Atlanta University; Together with the Proceedings of the Eighth Conference for the Study of the Negro Problems*, held at Atlanta University, 26 May 1903. Documenting the American South. The University of North Carolina at Chapel Hill.

________. 2003. *The Negro church*. New York: Altamira Press.

Durkheim, Emile. 1964. *The Division of Labor in Society*. New York: Free Press.

Eco, Umberto. 1976. *A Theory of Semiotics*, Bloomington: Indiana University Press.

Edwards, Korie L. 2008b. *The elusive dream: The power of race in interracial churches*. New York: Oxford University Press.

________. 2009. *Race, religion, and worship: Are contemporary African-American worship practices distinct? Journal for the Scientific Study of Religion* 48(1), 30-52.

Eliade, Mircea. 1959. *The Sacred and the Profane: The Nature of Religion* . Willard Trask (Trans.). New York: Harcourt, Brace & World.

________. 1969. *The quest for the 'origins' of religion. In The Quest: History and Meaning in Religion.* Chicago: University of Chicago Press.

________. 1961a. *Images and Symbols: Studies in Religious Symbolism.* London: Harvill Press.

________. 1961b. *The History of Religions and a New Humanism. History of Religions1*, 7-8.

Ellison, C. G. 1993. Religious Involvement and Self-Perception Among Black Americans. *Social Forces* 71(4), 1027-1055.

Ellison, Christoper, & Sherkat, Darren. 1991. The Politics of Black Religious Change: Disaffiliation from Black Mainline Denominations. *Social Forces* 70(2), 431-54.

________. 1995. The 'Semi-Involuntary Institution' Revisited: Regional Variations in Church Participation Among Black Americans. *Social Forces* 73(4), 1415-437.

Emerson, Michael O. 2006. *People of the dream: Multiracial congregations in the United States.* Princeton, NJ: Princeton University Press.

Emerson, Michael O. & Smith, Christian. 2000. *Divided by faith: Evangelical religion and the problem of race in America.* New York: Oxford University Press.

Fanon, Frantz. 1965. *The wretched of the earth.* New York: Grove Press.

________. 1967. *Black skin, white masks.* New York: Grove Press.

Fauconnier, Gilles & Turner, Mark. 2002. *The Way We Think.* New York: Basic Books.

Fauset, Arthur. 1971. The Negro and his religion. In: Hart M. Nelsen, Rayatha L. Yokley, & Anne K. Nelsen (Eds.), *The black church in America,* New York, Basic Books. pp. 163-174.

Feagin, Joe R. & Sikes, Melvin P. 1995. *Living with racism: The black middle-class experience.* Boston, MA: Beacon Press.

Felder, Cain Hope, (editor). 1991. *Stony the Road We Trod: African American Biblical Interpretation.* Fortress Press.

Fenton, Steve. 1999. *Ethnicity: Racism, class and culture.* Lanham, MD: Rowman & Littlefield.

Ferguson, L.G. 1991. Struggling with pots in colonial South Carolina. In: R.H. Mcguire & R, Paynter (Eds.), *The Archaeology of Inequality*, Oxford, Basil Blackwell, pp. 28-39.

________. 1992. *Uncommon Ground: Archeology and Early African America*, 1650-1800. Washington (DC): Smithsonian Institution Press.

Fett, Sharla. 2002. *Working Cures: Healing, Health, and Power on Southern Slave Plantations.* Chapel Hill: University of North Carolina Press.

Finke, R., & R. Stark. 1988. Religious economies and sacred canopies: Religious mobilization in American cities. *American Sociological Review* 53, 41-49.

________. 1992. *The churching of America*, 1776-1990: *Winners and losers in our religious economy.* New Brunswick, NJ: Rutgers University Press.

Fisch, Max H. 1986. *Peirce, Semeiotic, and Pragmatism,* In: Kenneth Laine Ketner & Christian J. W. Kloesel, Bloomington: Indiana University Press.

Fisher, Miles. 1953. *Negro Slave Songs in the United States*. New York: Citadel Press.

Foner, Eric.1988. *Reconstruction: America's Unfinished Revolution, 1863-1877.* New York: Harper Collins.

Forman, Robert K. C. 1999. *Mysticism, Mind, Consciousness*. New

York: State University of New York Press.

Foucault, Michel. 1972. *The Archaeology of Knowledge and The Discourse On Language*. A. M. Sheridan Smith (Trans.). New York: Pantheon.

Frazier, E. Franklin. 1964. *The Negro Church in America*. New York: Knopf.

Freeman, Howard E., David Armor, Michael J. Ross, & Thomas F. Pettigrew. 1966. Color gradation and attitudes among middle-income negroes. *American Sociological Review* 31(3), 365-74.

Fulop, Timothy E. 1991. The Future Golden Day of the Race: Millennialism and Black Americans in the Nadir, 1877-1901. *The Harvard Theological Review* 84(1), 75-99.

Gallup, George, & Jim Castelli. 1989. *The People's Religion: American Faith in the 90's*. Virginia: MacMillan.

Ganiel, Gladys. 2010. Ethnoreligious Change in Northern Ireland and Zimbabwe: A comparative study of how religious havens can have ethnic significance. *Ethnopolitics* 9(1), 103-20.

Genovese, Eugene D. 1976. *Roll, Jordan, Roll: The World the Slaves Made*. New York: Vintage Books.

Gibbs, Raymond. 1994. *The Poetics of Mind: Figurative Thought, Language and Understanding*. Cambridge: Cambridge University Press.

Gleiser, Marcelo.1998. *The Dancing Universe: From Creation Myths to the Big Bang,* New York: Dutton.

Goffman, Irving. 1974. *Frame Analysis*. Boston: Northeastern University Press.

Goudge, Thomas A. 1950. *The Thought of C. S. Peirce*. Toronto: Toronto University Press.

Grange, Joseph. 1994. Review of my Nature and Spirit: An Essay in Ecstatic Naturalism, *Society for the Advancement of American Philosophy Newsletter*, 68, 36-37.

Gregory, Steven. 1998. *Black Corona: Race and the Politics of Place in an Urban Community*. Princeton: Princeton University Press.

Gribin, John. 1993. *In the Beginning: After COBE and Before the Big Bang*, Boston: Little, Brown & Co.

Handler, J.S. & F.W. Lange, 1978. *Plantation Slavery in Barbados: An Archaeological and Historical Investigation.* Cambridge, MA: Harvard University Press.

Handler, J.S., F.W. Lange & C.E. Orser, Jr, 1979. Carnelian beads in necklaces from a slave cemetery in Barbados. *Ornament* 4(2), 15-18.

Hannerz, Ulf. 1969. *Soul side: Inquiries into Ghetto Culture and Community*. New York: Columbia University Press.

Hardwick, Charley D. 1996. *Events of Grace: Naturalism, Existentialism, and Theology*, Cambridge: Cambridge University Press.

Hardwick, Charley D. & Crosby, Donald A. 1997. *Pragmatism, Neo-Pragmatism, and Religion: Conservations with Richard Rorty, American Liberal Religious Thought.* New York: Peter Lang.

Harris, Fredrick C. 1999. *Something within: Religion in African-American political activism.* New York: Oxford University Press.

Harris, Michael. 1992. *The rise of gospel blues: The music of Thomas Andrew Dorsey in the urban church*. New York: Oxford University Press.

Harris, P., Lyon, D. & McLaughlin, S. 2005. *The Meaning of food.* Guilford, CT: The Globe Pequot Press.

Hartshorne, Charles. 1948. *The Divine Relativity: A Social Conception of God*, New Haven: Yale University Press.

________. 1962. *The Logic of Perfection and Other Essays in Neoclassical Metaphysics*, La Salle, IL: Open Court.

Harvey, Paul. 2005. That was about Equalization after Freedom: Southern Evangelicalism and the Politics of Reconstruction and Redemption, 1861-1900. In: Edward J. Blum & W. Scott Poole, *Vale of Tears: New Essays on Religion and Reconstruction*, Macon, GA: Mercer University Press.

Harvey, Van A. 1995. *Feuerbach and the Interpretation of Religion.* Cambridge: Cambridge University Press.

Hatcher, William E. 2000. John Jasper: The Unmatched Negro Philosopher and Preacher, *Documenting the American South.* University Library, The University of North Carolina at Chapel Hill, 2000. http://docsouth.unc.edu/church/hatcher/hatcher.html

Hausman, Carl R. 1993. *Charles S. Peirce's Evolutionary Philosophy*, Cambridge: Cambridge University Press.

Hawkes, Terence 1977. *Structuralism and Semiotics.* Berkeley: University of California Press.

Hawking, Stephen W. 1988. *A Brief History of Time.* New York: Bantam Books.

Hershman, D. Jablow & Lieb, Julian. 1988. *The Key to Genius: Manic- Depression and the Creative Life*, Buffalo, NY: Prometheus Books.

Herskovits, Melville J. 1970. *The myth of the Negro past.* Gloucester, MA: P. Smith.

Hill, Patricia Liggins, (ed). 1997. *Call and Response: The Riverside Anthology of the African American Literary Tradition.* Houghton: Mifflin Co.

Hill, R. B. 1997. *The strengths of African American families: Twenty-five years later.* Washington, D.C.: R & B Publishers.

Hinton, Mary. 2008 Saying Grace: Praying over the Loss of African-American Religious and Food Culture (and How They are Related). *Religious Education* 103(4), 469-479.

Holquist, Micheal. 1990. *Dialogism: Bakhtin and His World.* USA: Routledge.

Holt, John B. 1940. Holiness religion: Cultural shock and social reorganization. *American Sociological Review* 5, 740-747.

Hooks, Bell, & Cornel West. 1991. *Breaking bread: Insurgent Black intellectual life.* Boston: South End Press.

Hughes, Everett C. 1945. Dilemmas and Contradictions of Status. *American Journal of Sociology,* 50, 353-359.

Hughes, M. 1997. Soul food, black women, and food, In: Counihan, C. and Van Esterik, P.(Eds.) *Food and culture: A reader.* New York: Routledge.

Hunt, Larry L. & Matthew O. Hunt. 2001. Race, region, and religious involvement: A comparative study of whites and African Americans. *Social Forces* 80(2), 605-31.

Hunter, Margaret, Walter R. Allen, & Edward E. Telles, 2001. The significance of skin color among African Americans and Mexican Americans, *African American Research Perspectives*, 7(1), 173-184.

Irwin, Alexander C. 1991. *Eros Toward the World: Paul Tillich and the Theology of the Erotic.* Minneapolis: Fortress Press.

Jackson, J. S., Chatters, L. M., & Taylor, R. J. (Ed.). 1993. Aging in black America. Newbury Park, CA: Sage Publications.

Johnson, K.S., Elbert-Avila, K.I., & Tulsky, J. A. 2005. The Influence of Spiritual Beliefs and Practices on the treatment preferences of African-Americans: A review of the literature. *Journals of the American Geriatrics Society*, 53(4), 711-719.

Katz, Albert N., Cristina Cacciari, Raymond W. Gibbs, Jr., & Mark Turner. 1998. *Figurative Language and Thought. Counterpoints: Cognition, Memory, & Language*. New York: Oxford University Press.

Kauffman, Stuart. 1995. *At Home in the Universe: The Search for the Laws of Self-Organization and Complexity*, Oxford: Oxford University Press.

Kaut, Kevin Patrick, 2002. Religion, spirituality and existentialism near the end of life: Implications for assessment and application. *American Behavioral Scientist*, 46(2), 220-234

Kennedy, David. 1994. The Five Communities. *Analytic Teaching*, 15(1), 3-16.

Kerr, John. 1993. *A Most Dangerous Method: The Story of Jung, Freud, and Sabina Spielrein*. New York: Alfred A. Knopf.

Kövecses, Zóltan. 2002. *Metaphor: A Practical Introduction*. New York: Oxford University Press.

Krikorian, Yervant H. (ed). 1944. *Naturalism and the Human Spirit*. New York: Columbia University Press.

Kruse, Felicia E. 1990. Nature and Semiosis. *Transactions of the Charles S. Peirce Society*, 26(2), 211-224.

Laclau, Ernesto & Chantal Mouffe. 1985. *Hegemony and Socialist Strategy: Towards a Radical Democratic Politics*. London: Verso.

Lakoff, George & Johnson, Mark. 1980. *Metaphors We Live By*. Chicago and London: University of Chicago Press.

Leonard, Karen Isaksen. 1992. *Making ethnic choices: California's Punjabi Mexican Americans*, Philadelphia, PA: Temple University

Press.

Lenski, Gerhard. 1961. *The Religious Factor: A Sociological Study of Religion's Impact on Politics, Economics, and Family Life.* Doubleday & Co., Inc.

Levin, J.S., & Taylor, R. J. 1993. Gender and age differences in religiosity among black Americans, *Gerontologist*, 33, 16-23.

Levine, Lawrence. 1977. *Black Culture and Black Consciousness.* New York: Oxford University Press.

Lewis, Amanda E. 2004. What group? Studying whites and whiteness in the era of color blindness. *Sociological Theory* 22(4), 623-646.

Lightman, Alan. 1991. *Ancient Light: Our Changing View of the Universe.* Cambridge, MA: Harvard University Press.

Lincoln, C. Eric. 1974. *The Black Church Since Frazier.* New York: Schocken Books.

________. 1984. *Race, Religion and the Continuing American Dilemma.* New York: Hill and Wang.

Lincoln, C. Eric & Lawrence H. Mamiya. 1990. *The Black church in the African American experience.* Durham and London: Duke University Press.

Lipsitz, George. 1998. *The possessive investment in whiteness: How white people profit from identity politics.* USA: Temple University Press.

Litwack, Leon F. 1980. *Been in the Storm So Long: The Aftermath of Slavery.* New York: First Vintage Books Edition.

Logan, Rayford. 1954. *The Negro in American Life and Thought: The Nadir,* 1877-1901. New York: The Dial Press, Inc

Lovell, John. 1969. The Social Implications of the Negro Spiritual.

In: Bernard Katz (Ed)., *The Social Implications of Early Negro Music in the United States*, Arno Press, pp. 136-150.

Lukken, Gerard. 1994. *Per Visibilia ad Invisibilia: Anthropological, Theological, and Semiotic Studies on the Liturgy and the Sacraments*, *Kampen*, The Netherlands: Kok Pharos Publishing House.

Lutz, Norma J. 2001. *Jonathan Edwards: Colonial Religious Leader.* New York: Chelsea House Publications.

Mahoney, A., K. I. Pargament, N. Tarakeshwar, & A. B. Swank 2001. Religion in the Home in the 1980s and 90s: A Meta-Analytic Review and Conceptual Analyses of Links Between Religion, Marriage and Parenting. *Journal of Family Psychology* 15, 559-96.

Marable, Manning. 1995. Religion and Black Protest Thought in African American History. In: Gayraud Wilmore (Ed). *African American Religious Studies: An Interdisciplinary Anthology*. Duke University Press, pp. 318-39.

Maritain, Jacques. 1957. Language and the Theory of Sign. In: Ruth Nanda Anshen (Ed.), *Language: An Enquiry into its Meaning and Function*, New York, Harper & Row, pp. 86-101.

Marks, L. D., & C. Chaney 2006. *Faith Communities and African American Families: A Qualitative Look at Why the Black Church Matters.* In: S. D. Ambrose (Ed.), *Religion and Psychology: New Research,* Hauppauge, Nova Science Publishers, pp. 277-294.

Marks, L. D., M. Swanson, O. Nesteruk, & K. Hopkins-Williams 2006. Stressors in African American Marriages and Families: A Qualitative Study. *Stress, Trauma, and Crisis: An International Journal* 9, 203-225.

Marti, Gerardo. 2005. *A mosaic of believers: Diversity and innovation in a multiethnic church*. Bloomington, IN: Indiana University Press.

_______. 2008a. Fluid ethnicity and ethnic transcendence. *Journal for the Scientific Study of Religion* 47(1), 11-16.

_______. 2008b. *Hollywood faith: Holiness, prosperity, and ambition in a Los Angeles church*. New Brunswick, NJ: Rutgers University Press.

_______. 2009a. Affinity, identity, and transcendence: The experience of religious racial integration in multiracial churches. *Journal for the Scientific Study of Religion* 48(1), 53-68.

Marty, Martin E. 1984. *Pilgrims in their own land: 500 years of religion in America*. New York: Penguin Books.

Marx, G.T. 1967. *Protest and prejudice*. New York: Harper and Row.

Marx, Gary. 1971. Religion: Opiate or Inspiration of Civil Rights Militancy? In: Hart Nelsen, Raytha Yokley & Anne Nelsen (Eds.), *The Black Church in America*. Basic Books. pp. 50-60.

Marx, Karl. 1848[1977]. *The Marx-Engels Reader*. New York: Norton.

Massey Douglas S., & Nancy A. Denton. 1993. *American Apartheid: Segregation and the Making of the Underclass*. Boston: Harvard University Press.

Masuzawa, Tomoko. 1993. *In Search of Dreamtime: the Quest for the Origin of Religion*. Chicago: University of Chicago Press.

Mates, Benson. 1986. *The Philosophy of Leibniz: Metaphysics and Language*. New York: Oxford University Press.

Maton, P. E. 1989. Community Settings as Buffers of Life Stress? Highly Supportive Churches, Mutual Help Groups, and Senior Centers. *American Journal of Community Psychology* 17(2),

203-232.

Mattis, Jacqueline. S. 2000. African American Women's Definitions of Spirituality and Religiosity. *Journal of Black Psychology* 26(1), 101-122.

Mattis, Jacqueline S., Robert J. Jagers, Carrie A. Hatcher, G. Dawn Lawhon, Eleanor J. Murphy & Yohance F. Murray. 2000. Religiosity, volunteerism, and community involvement among African American men: An exploratory analysis. *Journal of community psychology,* 28(4), 391-406.

________. 2001. A relational framework for the study of religiosity and spirituality in the lives of African Americans. *Journal of Community Psychology* (Special Issue: Spirituality, Religion, and Community Psychology II: Resources, Pathways, and Perspectives) 29(5), 519-539.

________. 2002. The Role of Religion and Spirituality in the Coping Experience of African American Women: A Qualitative Analysis. *Psychological of Women Quarterly* 26, 308-320.

Mattis, J. S., Mitchell, N., Grayman, N.A, Zapata, A & Taylor R.J. 2007. Uses of Ministerial Support by African Americans: A Focus Group Study. *American Journal of Orthopsychiatry* 77(2), 249-258.

Mays, Benjamin & Joseph Nicholson. 1933. *The Negro's Church. Institute of Social and Religious Research.* New York: Institute of social and religious research

McAdoo, Harriette P. 1995. Stress Levels, Family Help Patterns, and Religiosity in Middle- and Working-Class African American Single Mothers. *Journal of Black Psychology,* 21(4), 424-449.

McCall, George & Jerry L. Simmons. 1978. *Identities and interactions: An examination of human associations in everyday life*. New York: Free Press.

Mcfague, Sallie. 1982. *Metaphorical Theology: Models of God*, Philadelphia: Fortress Press.

McKinney, William. 1998. Mainline Protestantism 2000. *Annals of the American Academy of political and Social Science* 558, 57-66.

McRoberts, Omar M. 2003. *Streets of Glory: Church and Community in a Black Urban Neighborhood.* Chicago, IL: The University of Chicago Press.

Meisner, Sanford & Longwell, Dennis. 1987. *On Acting.* New York: Vintage.

Merrell, Floyd. 1991. *Signs Becoming Signs: Our Perfusive, Pervasive Universe.* Bloomington: Indiana University Press.

Meshack, B. A. 1976. *Is the Baptist Church relevant to the Black community.* San Francisco: R & E Research Associates.

Miall, David S. 1995. Anticipation and feeling in literary response: A neuropsychological perspective. *Poetics* 23(4), 275-298.

Michael E. 1993. *Reflecting Black: African-American cultural criticism.* Minneapolis: University of Minnesota Press.

Mitchell, Henry H. 1970. *Black preaching.* Philadelphia, PA: J. P. Lippincott Company.

Mithen, Steven J. 1996. *The Prehistory of the Mind: The Cognitive Origins of Art, Religion and Science.* Cambridge: Cambridge University Press.

Montgomery, William E. 1993. *Under Their Own Vine and Fig Tree: The African-American Church in the South, 1865-1900.* Baton Rouge and London: Louisiana State University Press.

Moore, A. W. 1990. *The Infinite,* London: Routledge.

Moore, T. 1991. The African-American church: A source of

empowerment, mutual help, and social change. *Prevention in Human Services* 10, 147-167.

Moorhead, James. 1999. *World without End: Mainstream American Protestant Visions of the Last Things, 1880-1925*. Bloomington and Indianapolis: Indiana University Press.

Morgan, David L.(et.al). 1997. *Focus groups as qualitative research (2nd ed.)* Thousand oaks: Sage.

Morris, Aldon D. 1984. *The Origins of the Civil Rights Movement: Black Communities Organizing for Change*. Glencoe, IL: The Free Press.

Morris, Richard. 1993. *Cosmic Questions: Galactic Halos, Cold Dark Matter, and the End of Time.* New York: John Wiley & Sons.

Morton, L. 1941. *Robert Carter of Nomini hall: a Virginia tobacco planter of the eighteenth century.* Williamsburg, Va: Colonial Williamsburg Inc.

Moses, Wilson Jeremiah. 1978. *The Golden Age of Black Nationalism, 1850-1925*. New York : Oxford University Press.

________. 1989. *Alexander Crummell: A Study of Civilization and Discontent.* New York: Oxford University Press.

Murphy, Tim. 1999. The concept of Entwicklung in German Religionswissenschaft: Before and after Darwin. *Method & Theory in the Study of Religion* 11, 8-23.

________. 2000. Discourse. In: Willi Braun & Russell T. McCutcheon (Eds.), *Guide to the Study of Religion*. London: Cassell.

________. 2001. *Nietzsche, Metaphor, Religion*. Albany: State University of New York Press.

Myrdal, Gunnar. 1944. *An American dilemma: The negro problem and modern democracy*. New York: Harper & Bros.

Nagel, Joane. 1994. Constructing ethnicity: Creating and recreating ethnic identity and culture. *Social Problems* 41(1), 152-176.

________. 1996. *American Indian ethnic renewal : Red power and the resurgence of identity and culture.* New York: Oxford University Press.

Nasar, Sylvia. 1998. *A Beautiful Mind.* New York: Simon & Schuster.

Nelsen, Hart M. & Nelsen, Anne Kusener. 1975. *Black church in the sixties.* Lexington : University Press of Kentucky

Nelsen, Hart M. 1988. Unchurched Black Americans: Patterns of Religiosity and Affiliation. *Review of Religious Research* 29(4), 398-412.

Nelsen, Hart M. & Anne K. Nelsen. 1975. *The Black Church in the Sixties*. Lexington: University of Kentucky Press.

Nelson, J. R. 1996. Designing schools to meet the needs of students who exhibit disruptive behavior. *Journal of Emotional and Behavioral Disorders* 4(3), 147-161.

Nelson, Timothy J. 1996. Sacrifice of praise: Emotion and collective participation in an African-American worship service. *Sociology of Religion* 57(4), 379-396.

Nesher, Dan. 1984. Are There Grounds for Identifying 'Ground' with 'Interpretant' in Peirce's Pragmatic Theory of Meaning?, *Transactions of the Charles S. Peirce Society*, 20(3), 303-324.

Neville, Robert C. 1968. *God the Creator: On the Transcendence and Presence of God.* Chicago: University of Chicago Press.

________. 1981. *The Reconstruction of Thinking.* Albany: SUNY Press.

________. 1992. *God the Creator*. Albany: SUNY Press.

________. 1993. *Eternity and Time's Flow*. Albany: SUNY Press.

________. 1996. *The Truth of Broken Symbols*. Albany: SUNY Press.

________. 2001. *Symbols of Jesus: A Christology of Symbolic Engagement*. Cambridge: Cambridge University Press.

________. 2002. *Religion in Late Modernity*. Albany: SUNY Press.

________. 2006. *On the Scope and Truth of Theology: Theology as Symbolic Engagement*. New York: T&T Clark.

Newberg, Andrew, & Eugene D'Aquili e Vince Rause. 2001. *Why God Won't Go Away: Brain Science and the Biology of Belief.* New York: Ballentine Books.

Nichol, John T. 1971. *The Pentecostals*. Plainfield, NJ: Logos International.

Ogbu, John U. 1978. *Minority education and caste: The American system in cross-cultural perspective*. New York: Academic Press.

________. 1981. Origins of Human Competence: A Cultural-Ecological Perspective. *Child Development* 52(2), 413-429

Oliver, Kelly, ed. 1993a. *Ethics, Politics, and Difference in Julia Kristeva's Writing*. New York: Routledge.

Olmsted, K.A., Maluccio, A.N., & Fein,E. 1986. *Permanency planning for children: Concepts and methods*. Tavistock Publications.

Olson, Alan M. 1992. *Hegel and the Spirit: Philosophy as Pneumatology*. Princeton: Princeton University Press.

Omi, Michael A. & Howard Winant. 1994. *Racial formation in the United States*. New York: Routledge.

Orange, Donna. 1984. *Peirce's Conception of God: A Developmental*

Study, Lubbock, TX: Institute for Studies in Pragmaticism.

Orser, C.E., Jr, 1990. Archaeological approaches to New World plantation slavery. *Archaeological Method and Theory* 2, 111-54

Orser, Charles E. Owsley, Douglas W., & Shenkel, J. R. 1986. Gaining Access to New Orleans' First Cemetery. *Journal of Field Archaeology* 13(3), 342-345.

Pals, Daniel. 2009. *Introducing Religion: Readings from the Classic Theorists*. New York and Oxford: Oxford University Press.

Pargament, K. I. 1997 *The Psychology of Religion and Coping: Theory, Research, Practice*. New York: Guilford.

Pargament, K. I., & K. I. Maton 2000 *Religion in American Life: A Community Psychology Perspective (In Handbook of Community Psychology)*. New York: Kluwer Academic/ Plenum Publishers.

Paris, Peter J. 1995. *The Spirituality of African Peoples: The Search for a Common Moral Discourse*. Philadelphia: Fortress Press.

________. 2008. African American religion and public life: an assessment. *Association for Religion and Intellectual Life* 58(3), 475-494.

Park, Jerry Z., & Christian Smith. 2000. To Whom Much Has Been Given··· Religious Capital and Community Voluntarism Among Churchgoing Protestants. *Journal for the Scientific Study of Religion* 39(3), 272-286.

Patillo-McCoy,Mary. 1998. Church culture as a strategy of action in the black community. *American Sociological Review,* 63(6), 767-784.

Payne, P. 1954. Calabar Coronation. *The Nigerian Field* 19(2), 85-96.

Payne, P. 1969. Ibo Leaders Says Nigerian War in Final Phase.

Chicago Defender, 22-28.

Peirce, Charles S. 1977. *Semiotics and significs: the correspondence between Charles S. Peirce and Victoria* In: Lady Welby and C. S. Hardwick(Eds.). Bloomington: Indiana University.

________. 1998 [1893-1913]. *The essential Peirce: selected philosophical writings(Peirce Edition Project Vol 2).* Bloomington: Indiana University.

Perdue, Charles L., Jr., Barden, Thomas E. & Phillips, Robert K. 1976. *Weevils in the wheat: Interviews with Virginia ex-slaves.* Charlottesville, VA: University Press of Virginia.

Pierce, Lori., Yoo, David., & Spickard, Paul. 2001. Religion and Race: Korean and Japanese American Religions, 1890-1945. Paper presented at a meeting of the *Social Science Research Council Working Group on Religion and Immigration,* Seattle, WA.

Pierce, Yolanda. 2005. *Hell Without Fires: Slavery, Christianity, and the Antebellum SpiritualNarrative.* Gainesville: University Press of Florida.

Pilcher, George William. 1966. Samuel Davies and the Instruction of Negroes in Virginia. *The Virginia Magazine of History and Biography* 74(3), 293-300.

Pinn, Anthony B. 2002. *Black church in the post-civil rights era.* Maryknoll, NY: Orbis Books.

Pipes, Richard. 1970. *Struve, liberal on the left, 1870-1905.* Cambridge: Harvard University Press.

Pipes, William H. 1970. *Say amen, brother! Old-time Negro preaching: A study in American frustration.* Westport, CT: Negro Universities Press.

Pitts, Walter F. 1989. If you can't get the boat, take a log: Cultural interpretation in the Afro-Baptist ritual. *African Ethnologist* 16(2),

279-293.

________. 1993. *Old Ship of Zion: The Afro-Baptist Ritual in the African Diaspora.* New York: Oxford University Press.

Poloma, Margaret & George Gallup. 1991. *Varieties of Prayer.* Philadelphia: Trinity Press International.

Pope, Liston. 1942. *Millhands & preachers: A study of Gastonia.* New Haven, CT: Yale University Press.

Porter, Judith R. & Robert E. Washington. 1993. Minority identity and self-esteem. *Annual Review of Sociology* 19(1), 139-61.

Powell, LH., Shahabi, L., & Thoresen, CE. 2003. Religion and spirituality. Linkages to physical health. *Am Psychol* 58(1), 36-52

Progoff, Ira. 1956. *The Death and Rebirth of Psychology.* New York: McGraw-Hill.

________. 1973. *Synchronicity and Human Destiny.* New York: Delta.

Raboteau, Albert J. 1980[1978]. *Slave Religion: The "Invisible Institution" in the Ante-bellum South.* New York: Oxford University Press

________. 1995. *A Fire in the Bones: Reflections on African-American Religious History.* Boston: Beacon Press.

________. 1997. *African American Religion: Interpretive Essays in History and Culture.* New York: Routledge.

________. 1999. *Canaan Land: A Religious History of African Americans.* New York: Oxford University Press.

________. 1999. *African-American Religion.* New York: Oxford University Press.

________. 2000. The Rule of Gospel Order: Religious Life in the Slave Community. In: Larry G. Murphy (Ed.) *Down by the*

Riverside: Readings in African American Religion, New York: New York University Press.

________. 2002. *A Sorrowful Joy.* New York: Paulist Press.

Raposa, Michael L. 1989. *Peirce's Philosophy of Religion.* Bloomington: Indiana University Press

Rawick, George. 1972. God Struck Me Dead: Religious Conversion Experiences and Autobiographies of Negro Ex-Slaves. *Social Science Source Documents* 2. Nashville, Tenn.: Social Science Institute.

________. 1977. *The American Slave: A Composite Autobiography.* Georgia: Greenwood press.

Redkey, Edwin S. 1971. *Respect Black: The Writings and Speeches of Henry McNeal Turner.* New York: Arno Press and the New York Times.

Reich, Wilhelm. 1933. *Charakteranalyse, English translation of the third enlarged edition, Character Analysis.* Vincent R. Carfagno (Trans.), New York: The Noonday Press.

Robinson, Andrew, & Christopher Southgate. 2010. Semiotics as a Metaphysical Framework for Christian Theology. *Zygon: Journal of Religion and Science* 45, 689-712.

Robinson, Andrew. 2004. Continuity, Naturalism, and Contingency: A Theology of Evolution Drawing on the Semiotics of C. S. Peirce and Trinitarian Thought. *Zygon: Journal of Religion and Science* 39, 111-36.

Roof, W. C., & McKinney, W. 1987 *American Mainline Religion: Its Shape and Future.* New Brunswick: Rutgers University Press.

Rosen, C. C. 1982. Ethnic differences among impoverished rural elderly in use of religion as a coping mechanism. *Journal of Rural Community Psychology* 3, 27-34.

Royce, Anya Peterson. 1982. *Ethnic identity: Strategies of diversity.* Bloomington. IN: Indiana University Press.

Russell P. Spittler. 1999. Corinthian spirituality: How a flawed anthropology imperils authentic Christian existence. In: Edith L. Blumhofer, Russell P. Spittler and Grant A (Eds.), *Pentecostal currents in American Protestantism*, 3-19.

Ryder, John.1995. Review of my Nature and Spirit: An Essay in Ecstatic Naturalism. *Metaphilosophy* 26(1/2), 138-146.

Sack, D. 2000. *Whitebread Protestants: Food and religion in American culture.* New York: St. Martins Press.

Sanders, Jimy M. 2002. Ethnic boundaries and identity in plural societies. *Annual Review of Sociology* 28(1), 327-357.

Sawyer, Mary R. 2001. Theocratic, Prophetic, and Ecumenical: Political Roles of African American Clergy. In: Sue S. Crawford & Laura R. Olson (Eds.), *Christian Clergy in American Politics,* pp. 66-84.

Sebeok, Thomas A. 1991a. *Semiotics in the United States*, Bloomington: Indiana University Press.

_______. 1991b. *A Sign is Just a Sign.* Bloomington: Indiana University Press.

Sernett, Milton C. 1975. *Black religion and American evangelicalism: White Protestants, plantation missions, and the flowering of Negro Christianity, 1787-1865.* Metuchen, NJ: Scarecrow Press.

Seul, J. R. 1999. Ours is the Way of God: Religion, Identify, and Intergroup Conflict. *Journal of Peace Research* 36(5), 53-69.

Shea, William M. 1984. *The Naturalists and the Supernatural.* Macon, GA: Mercer University Press.

Sheriff, John K. 1989. *The Fate of Meaning: Charles Peirce, Structuralism, and Literature.* Princeton: Princeton University Press.

Sherkat, D. & Ellison, C.G. 1991. The politics of black religious change: Disaffiliation from black mainline denominations. *Social Forces* 70, 431-454.

Shults, F. L. 2010. Trinity, Time, and Church: A Response to the Theology of Robert W. Jenson. In: Colin E. Gunton (Ed.), *The Princeton Seminary bulletin,* 22(1), 95.

Shults, F. LeRon, & Andrea Hollingsworth. 2008. *The Holy Spirit.* Grand Rapids, Mich.: Eerdmans.

Shults, F. LeRon, & Steven Sandage. 2005. *Transforming Spirituality.* Grand Rapids, Mich.: Baker Academic.

Shults, F. LeRon. 2005. *Reforming the Doctrine of God.* Grand Rapids, Mich.: Eerdmans.

Singer, Milton. 1984. *Man's Glassy Essence: Explorations in Semiotic Anthropology.* Bloomington: Indiana University Press.

Smith, Jonathan Z. 1982. *Sacred persistence: Towards a redescription of canon. In Imagining Religion: From Babylon to Jonestown.* Chicago: University of Chicago Press.

Smoot, George & Davidson, Keay. 1993. *Wrinkles in Time.* New York: William Morrow & Co.

Snow, David, E. Burke Rochford Jr., Steven Worden & Robert Benford. 1986. Frame Alignment Processes, Micromobilization and Movement Participation. *American Sociological Review* 51, 464-481.

Soler, J. 1997. The semiotics of food in the Bible. In: Counihan, C. and Van Esterik, P. (Eds.), *Food and culture: A reader.* New York, Routledge, PP. 55-66.

Sollors, Werner. 1989. *The Invention of ethnicity.* New York: Oxford University Press.

Southern, Eileen 1991. The antebellum church. *Black American Literature Forum* 25(1), 22.

Southgate, Christopher, & Andrew Robinson. 2010. Interpretation and the Origin of Life. *Zygon: Journal of Religion and Science* 45, 345-360.

Spiegelberg, Herbert. 1982. *The Phenomenological Movement: A Historical Introduction.* The Hague: Martinus Nijhoff.

Steele, Shelby. 1990. *Content of our character: A new vision of race in America.* New York: St. Martin's Press.

Steensland, Brian. Jerry Z. Park, Mark D. Regnerus, Lynn D. Robinson, W. Bradford Wilcox, & Robert D. Woodberry. 2000. The measure of American religion: Toward improving the state of the art. *Social Forces* 79(1), 291-318.

Stein, Murray. 1995. *The Interactive Field in Analysis.* Wilmette, IL: Chiron Publishers.

Stewart, Carlyle F. 1997. *Soul survivors: An African American spirituality.* Louisville, KY: Westminster John Knox Press.

Stryker, Sheldon. 1981. Symbolic interactionism: Themes and variations. In: Morris Rosenburg and Ralph H. Turner (Eds.), *Social psychology: Sociological perspectives,* New York, Basic, pp. 3-29.

Swain, R. D. 2008. Standing on the promises that cannot fail: Evaluating the Black Church's ability to promote community activism among African Americans in the present day context. *Journal of African American Studies,* 4(12), 401-413.

Sweet, William W. 1952. *The Puritan Heritage.* By George M. Stephenson. New York: Macmillan

Sweetser, Eve. 1991. *From Etymology to Pragmatics: Metaphorical and Cultural Aspects of Semantic Structure.* Cambridge: Cambridge University Press.

Swidler, Ann. 1986. Culture in action: Symbols and Strategies. *American Sociological Review* 51(2), 273-286.

________. 1995. Cultural Power and Social Movements. In: Hank Johnston and Bert Klandermans (Eds.). *Social Movements and Culture,* Vol. 4., University of Minnesota Press, pp. 25-40.

Synan, Vinson. 1971. *The Holiness-Pentecostal movement in the United States.* Grand Rapids, MI: Eerdmans Press.

Takaki, Ronald. 1979. *Iron cages: race and culture in 19th century America.* New York: Oxford University Press.

Taylor, Clarence. 1994. *The Black Churches of Brooklyn.* New York: Columbia University Press.

Taylor, J. T., Chatters, L. M., & Levin, J. S., 1995. A Multidimensional Measure of Religious Involvement for African Americans. *Sociological Quarterly* 36, 157-73.

Taylor, J. T., Ellison, C. G., Chatters, L. M., Levin, J. S., & Lincoln, K. D. 2000. Mental Health Services in Faith Communities: The Role of Clergy in Black Churches. *Social Work* 45(1), 73-86.

Taylor, R. B. 1999. The Incivilities thesis: Theory, measurement, and policy. In: R. H. Langworthy (Ed.), *Measuring What Matters.* Washington, D.C., National Institute of Justice/Office of Community Oriented Policing Services. pp 65-88.

Taylor, R. B., Jackson, J. S., & Chatters, L. M. 1997. *Family Life in Black America.* Thousand Oaks, CA: Sage.

Taylor, R. J. 1988. Correlates of Religious Non-Involvement among Black Americans. *Review of Religious Research* 30, 126-139.

Taylor, R. J., Thorton, M. C. & Chatters, 1988. Black American's perception of the sociohistoric role of the church. *Journal of Black Studies*, 18(2), 123-138.

Taylor, R. J, Chatters, L. M., Mattis, J. S., & Joe, S. 2000. Religious Involvement among Caribbean Blacks in the United States. *Review of religious research,* 52(2), 125-145.

Taylor, R. J., Chatters, L. M & Levin, J. 2004. *Religion in the Lives of African Americans: Social, Psychological, and Health Perspectives.* Thousand Oaks, CA: Sage.

Taylor, R. J. & Chatters, L.M. 1991. Religious life. In J. S. Jackson (Ed.), *Life in Black America*, Newbory Park, CA, Sage, pp. 105-123.

Taylor, Sage. R. J. 1988. Structural Determinants of Religious Participation Among Black Americans. *Review of Religious Research* 30, 114-25.

Thomas, S., Quinn, S., Billingsley, A., & Caldwell, C. 1994. The characteristics of Northern Black churches with community health outreach programs. *American Journal of Public Health,* 84(4), 575-579.

Thompson, Eric & Hartmann, Douglas. 2008. Critical whiteness theories and the evangelical "race problem": Extending Emerson and Smith's Divided by faith. *Journal for the Scientific Study of Religion* 47(3), 341-59.

Tillich, Paul. 1925[1973]. *Religions philosophie in Lehrbuch der Philosophie.* Berlin: Ullstein.

________. 1951. *Systematic Theology*, Vol. I. Chicago: University of Chicago Press.

________. 1952. *The Courage to Be*, New Haven: Yale University Press.

________. 1957. *Systematic Theology,* Vol. II. Chicago: University of Chicago Press.

________. 1963. *Systematic Theology,* Vol. III. Chicago: University of Chicago Press.

Torrance, Robert M. 1994. *The Spiritual Quest: Transcendence in Myth, Religion, and Science.* Berkeley: University of California Press.

Tsur, Reuven. 2003. *On the Shore of Nothingness: Space, Rhythm, and Semantic Structure in Religious Poetry and Its Mystic-Secular Counterpart. A Study in Cognitive Poetics.* Thorverton: Imprint Academic.

Tuan, Mia. 1998. *Forever foreigners or honorary whites? The Asian ethnic experience today*. New Brunswick, NJ: Rutgers.

Turner, Mark. 1996. *The literary mind: The origins of thought and language.* New York: Oxford University Press.

Verba, Sidney, Kay Lehman Schlozman & Henry Brady. 1993. Race, Ethnicity, and Political Resources: Participation in United States. *British Journal of Political Science* 23, 453-97.

Verna M,Keith, Verna M & Herring, Cedric. 1991. Skin tone and stratification in the black community. *The American Journal of Sociology [AJS]*, 97, 760-778.

Vigil, James Diego. 1998. *From Indians to Chicanos: The dynamics of Mexican-American culture.* Prospect Heights, IL: Waveland Press.

Wallace, Maurice O. 2009. *A Noble Fight: African American Freemasonry and the Struggle for Democracy in America*. Urbana: University of Illinois Press.

Warner , R. Stephen. 1988. *New wine in old wineskins: Evangelicals and liberals in a small-town church.* Berkeley, CA: University of California Press.

Warner, Julian 1993. Writing and Literary Work in Copyright: a Binational and Historical analysis. *Journal of the American Society for Information Science,* 307-321.

Washington, Booker T. 1971. *The Future of the American Negro.* Boston: Small, Maynard & Company.

Weber, M. 1964. T*he Theory of Social and Economic Organization.* Toronto: Free Press.

Weber, Max. 1930. *The Protestant Ethic and the Spirit of Capitalism.* Los Angeles: Roxbury Publishing Company.

_______. 1946. *From Max Weber: Essays in Sociology.* Oxford University Press.

West, Cornel. 1929b(1978). *Process and Reality.* New York: Macmillan.

_______. 1982. *Prophecy Deliverance: An Afro-American Revolutionary Christianity.* Philadelphia: Westminster Press.

_______. 1989. *The American Evasion of Philosophy: A Genealogy of Pragmatism.* Madison, WI: The University of Wisconsin Press.

_______. 1993. *Race Matters.* Boston: Beacon Press.

Whitehead, Alfred, North. 1929a. *The Function of Reason.* Boston: Beacon Press.

White, J. 1998. *Soul food: Recipes and reflections from African-American churches.* New York, NY: Harper Collins Publishers William Morrow Cookbooks.

Whitmond, Edward C. & Perera, Sylvia Brinton. 1989. *Dreams, A Portal to the Source.* London: Routledge.

Wiley, A., H. Warren, & D. S. Montanelli. 2002. Shelter in a Time of Storm: Parenting in Two Poor, Rural African American Communities. *Family Relations* 51, 265-73.

Williams, M. 1974. *Community in a Black Pentecostal Church-An Anthropological Study.* Pennsylvania: University of Pittsburgh Press.

Williamson, W. & Kautz, D. 2009. "Let's get moving: Let's get praising:" Promoting health and hope in an African American church. *The ABNF Journal*, 20(4), 2-105.

Wilmore, Gayraud S. 1994. *Black Religion and Black Radicalism: An Interpretation of the Religious History of Afro-American People.*

Maryknoll, N.Y: Orbis Books.

________. 1995. *African American Religious Studies: An Interdisciplinary Anthology.* Durham: Duke University Press.

Wilson, John & Harvey K. Clow. 1981. Themes of power and control in a Pentecostal assembly. *Journal for the Scientific Study of Religion* 20(3), 241-50.

Wilson, William Julius. 1986. *The Truly Disadvantaged: The Inner City, the Underclass, and Public Policy.* Chicago: University of Chicago Press.

Wind, J. P., & J. W. Lewis. 1994. *American Congregations: Volume 1: Portraits of Twelve Religious Communities.* Chicago: University of Chicago Press.

Yancey, George. 2003a. *Who is white? Latinos, Asians, and the new black/nonblack divide.* Boulder, CO: Lynne Rienner.

Yinger, John. 1995. *Closed doors opportunities lost.* New York: Russel Sage Foundation.

Young, V. H. 1970. Family and Childhood in a Southern Negro Community. *American Anthropologist* 72, 269-288.

Index

[A]

[B]

[C]

[D]

[E]

[J]

[K]

[L]

[M]

[N]

[O]

[P]

[Q]

[R]

[S]

[T]

[U]

[V]

[W]

[Y]